*Prolegomena to a*
*Theory of Language*

# PROLEGOMENA *to a*
# *Theory of Language*

BY LOUIS HJELMSLEV

*Translated by Francis J. Whitfield*

THE UNIVERSITY OF WISCONSIN PRESS
*Madison, 1963*

P
105
.H514
1961

*Published by*
THE UNIVERSITY OF WISCONSIN PRESS
*430 Sterling Court, Madison 6, Wisconsin*

*Revised English edition © 1961 by the*
*Regents of the University of Wisconsin*

*Second Printing, 1963*

*Printed in the United States of America*
*by George Banta Company, Inc.,*
*Menasha, Wisconsin*

*Library of Congress Catalog Card Number 62-7095*

# PREFACE

The original version of the present work appeared in 1943 under the title *Omkring sprogteoriens grundlæggelse.** The pagination of that edition is given at the left margin of this volume. The English translation was first published in 1953 as Memoir 7 of the *International Journal of American Linguistics (Indiana University Publications in Anthropology and Linguistics)*. This second, revised edition incorporates several minor corrections and changes that have suggested themselves in the course of discussions between the author and the translator. For the development of the theory in recent years, the reader may be referred particularly to the author's study *La stratification du langage*, reprinted in his *Essais linguistiques (Travaux du Cercle linguistique de Copenhague*, XII, Copenhagen, Nordisk Sprog- og Kulturforlag, 1959), which include other articles on linguistic theory by the same author and a complete bibliography.

L. Hj.
F.J.W.

* *Festskrift udgivet af Københavns Universitet i anledning af Universitetets Aarsfest, November 1943*, pp. [3]–[113]; also published separately by Ejnar Munksgaard, Copenhagen, 1943.

# CONTENTS

*Prolegomena to a*
  *Theory of Language*

Language—human speech—is an inexhaustible abundance of manifold treasures. Language is inseparable from man and follows him in all his works. Language is the instrument with which man forms thought and feeling, mood, aspiration, will and act, the instrument by whose means he influences and is influenced, the ultimate and deepest foundation of human society. But it is also the ultimate, indispensable sustainer of the human individual, his refuge in hours of loneliness, when the mind wrestles with existence and the conflict is resolved in the monologue of the poet and the thinker. Before the first awakening of our consciousness language was echoing about us, ready to close around our first tender seed of thought and to accompany us inseparably through life, from the simple activities of everyday living to our most sublime and intimate moments—those moments from which we borrow warmth and strength for our daily life through that hold of memory that language itself gives us. But language is no external accompaniment. It lies deep in the mind of man, a wealth of memories inherited by the individual and the tribe, a vigilant conscience that reminds and warns. And speech is the distinctive mark of the personality, for good and ill, the distinctive mark of home and of nation, mankind's patent of nobility. So inextricably has language grown inside personality, home, nation, mankind, and life itself that we may sometimes be tempted to ask whether language is a mere reflexion of, or simply *is* not all those things—the very seed leaf of their growth.

For these reasons language has attracted man as an object for wonderment and for description, in poetry and in science. Science has been led to see in language series of sounds and expressive

3

6]        gestures, amenable to exact physical and physiological
          description, and ordered as signs for the phenomena of
consciousness. It has sought in language, through psychological and logical interpretations, the fluctuation of the human
psyche and the constancy of human thought—the former in the
capricious life and change of language, the latter in its signs, of
which two kinds were recognized, the word and the sentence, the
palpable symbols of concept and judgment respectively. Language, conceived as a sign system and as a stable entity, was
expected to provide the key to the system of human thought, to
the nature of the human psyche. Conceived as a super-individual
social institution, it was to contribute to a characterization of
the nation. Conceived as a fluctuating and changing phenomenon, it was to open the door to an understanding both of the
style of the personality and of the distant vicissitudes of bygone
generations. Language came to be looked upon as a key position
from which vistas might be opened in many directions.

Considered thus, language, even when it is the object of scientific investigation, becomes not an end in itself, but a means:
means to a knowledge whose main object lies outside language itself, although it is perhaps fully attainable only through language, and which can be gained only on other assumptions than
those implied by language. Here language is a means to a transcendent knowledge (in the proper and etymological sense of the
word *transcendent*), not the goal of an immanent knowledge. Thus
the physical and physiological description of speech-sounds easily
degenerates into pure physics and pure physiology, and the psychological and logical description of signs (words and sentences)
into pure psychology, logic, and ontology, so that the linguistic
point of departure is lost from view. This is confirmed by the
experience of history. But even where this is not directly the
case, still the physical, physiological, psychological, and logical
phenomena *per se* are not language itself, but only disconnected,
external facets of it, selected as objects of study, not for language's sake, but for the sake of the phenomena towards which

language is oriented. The same holds true when language is further considered, on the basis of these descriptions, as a key to the understanding of social conditions and to the reconstruction of prehistoric relations among peoples and nations.

This is not said to minimize the value of all these points of view and all these efforts, but to point out a danger: the danger that in our zealous haste towards the goal of our knowledge we may overlook the means of knowledge—language itself. The danger is a real one because it is in the nature of language to be overlooked, to be a means and not an end, and it is only by artifice that the searchlight can be directed on the means of knowledge itself. This is true in daily life, where language normally does not come to consciousness; but it is equally true in scientific research. It was long ago understood that in addition to philology—the study of language and its texts as a means to literary and historical insight—it must be possible to have a linguistics, a study of language and its texts as an end in itself. But it was a long way from plan to execution. Once more, language disappointed its scientific suitors. What came to make up the main content of conventional linguistics —linguistic history and the genetic comparison of languages— had neither as aim nor as result a knowledge of the nature of language, but rather a knowledge of historical and prehistorical social conditions and contacts among peoples, a knowledge obtained through language taken as a means. But this, too, is philology. It is true that in the inner technique of this kind of comparative linguistics we often seem to be studying language itself, but that is an illusion. We are really studying the *disiecta membra* of language, which do not permit us to grasp the totality that language is. We are studying the physical and physiological, psychological and logical, sociological and historical precipitations of language, not language itself.

To establish a true linguistics, which cannot be a mere ancillary or derivative science, something else must be done. Linguistics must attempt to grasp language, not as a conglomerate of non-linguistic (*e.g.*, physical, physiological, psychological, logical, sociological) phenomena, but as a self-sufficient totality, a structure *sui generis*. Only in this way can language in itself be subjected to scientific treatment without again disappointing its investigators and escaping their view.

In the long run it must be possible to measure the significance of doing this by the repercussions that such a linguistics must have on the various transcendent points of view—on the philologies and on what has till now been considered linguistics. In particular, through the theory of such a linguistics it should be possible to provide a uniform basis of comparison between languages by removing that provincialism in the formation of concepts that is the pitfall of the philologist and thus eventually to establish a real and rational genetic linguistics. In its more immediate consequences, the significance of such a linguistics
8]    —whether the structure of language be equated with that of reality or be taken as a more or less distorted reflexion of it—may also be measured by its contributions to general epistemology.

What is required is the construction of a linguistic theory that will discover and formulate the premises of such a linguistics, establish its methods, and indicate its paths.

The present work constitutes the prolegomena to such a theory.

The study of language, with its multifarious, essentially transcendent aims, has many cultivators; the theory of language, with its purely immanent aim, few. In this connexion, the theory of language must not be confused with the philosophy of language. Like the history of any other discipline, the history of the study of language has witnessed attempts to give philosophical motivations for actual practices of investigation, and, in connexion with the interest in foundations that has been growing in recent years, certain transcendent kinds of linguistics have been provided with their presumed systems of axioms.[1] At the same time,

---

[1] Leonard Bloomfield, "A set of postulates for the science of language" (*Language* II, 1926, pp. 153–164).—Karl Bühler, *Sprachtheorie*, Jena, 1934. *Id.*,

it is very seldom that these speculations of linguistic philosophy assume such an apparently exact form, or that they are systematically undertaken on any large scale by investigators with sufficient preparation in both linguistics and epistemology. Most of them can be relegated to the category of subjective speculation, and therefore none of them has won much approval—except perhaps temporarily, as relatively superficial trends of fashion. For this reason the history of linguistic theory cannot be written and its evolution cannot be followed—it is too discontinuous. Because of this situation, attempts to form a linguistic theory have been discredited by many as empty philosophizing and dilettantism, characterized by apriorism. The condemnation seems even justified, since dilettantish and aprioristic philosophizing has actually prevailed in this field to such an extent as to make it difficult to distinguish, from the outside, between the true and the false. A possible contribution of the present work should be to make clear that these characteristics are not an inherent necessity in any attempt at a linguistic theory. We shall best achieve this aim by forgetting the past, to a certain degree, and by starting from the beginning in all cases where the past has yielded nothing of positive usefulness. To a large extent we shall build on the same empirical material as that investigated in previous research, material which, in reinterpreted form, constitutes the object of linguistic theory. We shall 9] explicitly acknowledge our indebtedness where we know the results to have been reached by others before us. One linguistic theoretician should be singled out as an obvious pioneer: the Swiss, Ferdinand de Saussure.[2]

Preparatory work of essential importance to the linguistic theory here presented was done in collaboration with certain members of the Linguistic Circle of Copenhagen, notably with

---

"Die Axiomatik der Sprachwissenschaften" (*Kantstudien* XXXVIII, 1933, pp. 19–90).

[2] Ferdinand de Saussure, *Cours de linguistique générale*, publ. par Ch. Bally & Alb. Sechehaye, Paris, 1916; 2nd ed., 1922; 3rd ed., 1931, 1949.

H. J. Uldall, in the years 1934–1939. In the elaboration of some of the basic assumptions of the theory the author profited from discussions in the Copenhagen Philosophical and Psychological Society and, besides, from a more detailed exchange of thought with Jørgen Jørgensen and Edgar Tranekjær Rasmussen. The responsibility for the present work is the author's alone.

## 2. *Linguistic theory and humanism*

A linguistic theory which searches for the specific structure of language through an exclusively formal system of premises must, while continually taking account of the fluctuations and changes of speech, necessarily refuse to grant exclusive significance to those changes; it must seek a *constancy*, which is not anchored in some "reality" outside language—a constancy that makes a language a language, whatever language it may be, and that makes a particular language identical with itself in all its various manifestations. When this constancy has been found and described, it may then be projected on the "reality" outside language, of whatever sort that "reality" may be (physical, physiological, psychological, logical, ontological), so that, even in the consideration of that "reality," language as the central point of reference remains the chief object—and not as a conglomerate, but as an organized totality with linguistic structure as the dominating principle.

The search for such an aggregating and integrating constancy is sure to be opposed by a certain humanistic tradition which, in various dress, has till now predominated in linguistic science. In its typical form this humanistic tradition denies *a priori* the existence of the constancy and the legitimacy of seeking it. According to this view, humanistic, as opposed to natural, phenomena are non-recurrent and for that very reason cannot, like natural phenomena, be subjected to exact and generalizing treatment. In the field of the humanities, consequently, 10] there would have to be a different method—namely, mere description, which would be nearer to poetry than to exact science—or, at any event, a method that restricts itself to a discursive form of presentation, in which the phenomena pass by, one by one, without being interpreted through a system. In the field of *history* this thesis has been held as doctrine, and it seems in fact to be the very basis of history in its classical form. Accordingly, those disciplines that may perhaps be called most humanistic—the study of literature and the study of art—have also been historically descriptive rather than systematizing disciplines. In certain fields a tendency to systematize may be observed, but history and, along with it, the humanities as a whole still seem to be far from willing to recognize the legitimacy and possibility of any such systematization.

*A priori* it would seem to be a generally valid thesis that for every *process* there is a corresponding *system*, by which the process can be analyzed and described by means of a limited number of premises. It must be assumed that any process can be analyzed into a limited number of elements recurring in various combinations. Then, on the basis of this analysis, it should be possible to order these elements into classes according to their possibilities of combination. And it should be further possible to set up a general and exhaustive calculus of the possible combinations. A history so established should rise above the level of mere primitive description to that of a systematic, exact, and generalizing science, in the theory of which all events (possible combinations of elements) are foreseen and the conditions for their realization established.

It seems incontestable that, so long as the humanities have not tested this thesis as a working hypothesis, they have neglected their most important task, that of seeking to establish the humanistic studies as a science. It should be understood that the description of humanistic phenomena must choose between, on the one hand, poetic treatment alone as the only possible treatment and, on the other hand, poetic and scientific treatment as two coordinate forms of description; and it should also be understood that the choice hinges on testing the thesis that a process has an underlying system.

11]      It would seem *a priori* that language is an object on
which this thesis might be tested with an expectation of
a positive result. A mere discursive description of linguistic
events cannot possibly arouse sufficient interest, and the need for
a supplementary, systematizing point of view has therefore always been felt: behind the textual process have been sought a
phonetic system, a semantic system, a grammatical system. But
until now, linguistic science, cultivated by philologists with a
transcendent objective and under the strong influence of a human-
ism that has rejected the idea of system, has failed to carry the
analysis through to the end, to make its premises clear, or to
strive for a uniform principle of analysis, and it has therefore
remained vague and subjective, metaphysical and æstheticizing,
to say nothing of those many occasions when it has entrenched
itself in a completely anecdotal form of presentation.

It is the aim of linguistic theory to test, on what seems a particularly inviting object, the thesis that a process has an underlying system—a fluctuation an underlying constancy. Voices
raised beforehand against such an attempt in the field of the
humanities, pleading that we cannot subject to scientific analysis
man's spiritual life and the phenomena it implies without killing
that life and consequently allowing our object to escape consideration, are merely aprioristic, and cannot restrain science from
the attempt. If the attempt fails—not in particular perform-
ances, but in principle—then these objections are valid, and
humanistic phenomena can be treated only subjectively and
æsthetically. If, however, the attempt succeeds—so that the
principle shows itself practicable—then these voices will become
silent of their own accord, and it would then remain to perform
corresponding experiments in the other fields of the humanities.

## 3. *Linguistic theory and empiricism*

A theory will attain its simplest form by building on no other
premises than those necessarily required by its object. More-

over, in order to conform to its purpose, a theory must be capable of yielding, in all its applications, results that agree with so-called (actual or presumed) empirical data.

At this point, every theory is faced with a methodological requirement, whose purport will have to be investigated by epistemology. Such an investigation may, we think, be omitted here.

We believe that the requirement we have vaguely formu-
12] lated above, the requirement of so-called empiricism, will
be satisfied by the principle that follows. By this principle, which we set above all others, our theory is at once clearly distinguishable from all previous undertakings of linguistic philosophy:

*The description shall be free of contradiction (self-consistent), exhaustive, and as simple as possible. The requirement of freedom from contradiction takes precedence over the requirement of exhaustive description. The requirement of exhaustive description takes precedence over the requirement of simplicity.*

We venture to call this principle the *empirical principle*. But we are willing to abandon the name if epistemological investigation shows it to be inappropriate. From our point of view this is merely a question of terminology, which does not affect the maintenance of the principle.

## 4. Linguistic theory and induction

The assertion of our so-called empirical principle is not the same as an assertion of inductivism, understood as the requirement of a gradual ascent from something particular to something general, or from something more limited to something less limited. Here again we are in the realm of terms that require epistemological analysis and refinement, this time terms which we ourself shall later have occasion to apply more precisely than we can here. And here again, both now and later, a terminological reckoning remains to be made with epistemology. For the time being we are interested in clarifying our position as opposed to that of previous linguistics. In its typical form this linguistics ascends, in its formation of concepts, from the individual sounds to the phonemes (classes of sounds), from the individual phonemes to the categories of phonemes, from the various individual meanings to the general or basic meanings, and from these to the categories of meanings. In linguistics, we usually call this method of procedure *inductive*. It may be defined briefly as a progression from component to class, not from class to component. It is a synthetic, not an analytic, movement, a generalizing, not a specifying, method.

Experience alone is sufficient to demonstrate the obvious shortcomings of this method. It inevitably leads to the abstraction of concepts which are then hypostatized as real. This realism (in the mediæval sense of the word) fails to yield a useful basis of comparison, since the concepts thus obtained are not general and are therefore not generalizable beyond a single language in an individual stage. All our inherited terminology suffers from this unsuccessful realism. The class concepts of grammar that are obtained by induction, such as "genitive," "perfect," "subjunctive," "passive," *etc.*, afford striking examples of this fact. None of them, as used till now, is susceptible of general definition: genitive, perfect, subjunctive, and passive are quite different things in one language, Latin for example, from what they are in another, say Greek. The same is true, without any exception, of the remaining concepts of conventional linguistics. In this field, therefore, induction leads from fluctuation, not to constancy, but to accident. It therefore finally comes in conflict with our empirical principle: it cannot ensure a self-consistent and simple description.

If we start from the supposed empirical data, these very data will impose the opposite procedure. If the linguistic investigator is given anything (we put this in conditional form for epistemological reasons), it is the as yet unanalyzed *text* in its undivided and absolute integrity. Our only possible procedure, if we wish to order a system to the process of that text, will be an analysis, in which the text is regarded as a class analyzed into components, then these components as classes analyzed into components, and so on until the analysis is exhausted. This procedure may therefore be defined briefly as a progression from class to component, not from component to class, as an analytic and specifying, not a synthetic and generalizing, movement, as the opposite of induction in the sense established in linguistics. In recent linguistics, where the contrast has been actualized, this method of procedure or an approximation thereto has been designated by the word *deduction*. This usage disturbs epistemologists, but we retain it here since we believe we shall later be able to demonstrate that the terminological opposition on this point is not insuperable.

## 5. *Linguistic theory and reality*

With the terminology that we have chosen, we have been able to designate the method of linguistic theory as necessarily empirical and necessarily deductive, and we have thus been able to cast light from one direction on the primitive and immediate question of the relation of linguistic theory to the so-called empirical data. But we still have to cast light on the same

14] question from another direction. That is to say, we must investigate to see whether the possible influences between the theory and its object (or objects) are reciprocal or unidirectional. To formulate the problem in a simplified, tendentious, and deliberately naive form—does the object determine and affect the theory, or does the theory determine and affect its object?

Here too, we must set aside the purely epistemological problem in its entire scope and restrict our attention to that aspect of it which directly concerns us. It is clear that the frequently misused and disparaged word *theory* can be taken in different senses. *Theory* can mean, among other things, a system of hypotheses. If the word is taken in this—now frequent—sense, it is clear that the influence between theory and object is unidirectional: the object determines and affects the theory, not *vice versa*.

Hypotheses can be shown to be true or false by a process of verification. But it may have already been apparent that we are using the word *theory* in another sense. In this connexion, two factors are of equal importance:

1. A theory, in our sense, is in itself independent of any experience. In itself, it says nothing at all about the possibility of its application and relation to empirical data. It includes no existence postulate. It constitutes what has been called a purely deductive system, in the sense that it may be used alone to compute the possibilities that follow from its premisses.

2. A theory introduces certain premisses concerning which the theoretician knows from preceding experience that they fulfil the conditions for application to certain empirical data. These premisses are of the greatest possible generality and may therefore be able to satisfy the conditions for application to a large number of empirical data.

The first of these factors we shall call the *arbitrariness* of a theory; the second we shall call its *appropriateness*. It seems necessary to consider both these factors in the preparation of a theory, but it follows from what has been said that the empirical data can never strengthen or weaken the theory itself, but only its applicability.

A theory permits us to deduce theorems, which must all have the form of implications (in the logical sense) or must be susceptible of transposition into such a conditional form. 15] Such a theorem asserts only that if a condition is fulfilled the truth of a given proposition follows. In the application of the theory it will become manifest whether the condition is fulfilled in any given instance.

On the basis of a theory and its theorems we may construct hypotheses (including the so-called laws), the fate of which, contrary to that of the theory itself, depends exclusively on verification.

No mention has been made here of axioms or postulates. We

leave it to epistemology to decide whether the basic premisses explicitly introduced by our linguistic theory need any further axiomatic foundation. In any event, they are traced back so far and they are all of so general a nature that none would seem to be specific to linguistic theory as opposed to other theories. This is done because our aim is precisely to make clear our premisses as far back as we can without going beyond what seems directly appropriate to linguistic theory. We are thereby forced in some degree to invade the domain of epistemology, as has appeared in the preceding sections. Our procedure here is based on the conviction that it is impossible to elaborate the theory of a particular science without an active collaboration with epistemology.

Linguistic theory, then, sovereignly defines its object by an arbitrary and appropriate strategy of premisses. The theory consists of a calculation from the fewest and most general possible premisses, of which none that is specific to the theory seems to be of axiomatic nature. The calculation permits the prediction of possibilities, but says nothing about their realization. Thus, if linguistic theory, taken in this sense, is set in relation to the concept of reality, the answer to our question, whether the object determines and affects the theory or *vice versa*, is "both . . . and": by virtue of its arbitrary nature the theory is *arealistic;* by virtue of its appropriateness it is *realistic* (with the word *realism* taken here in the modern, and not, as before, in the mediæval sense).

## 6. The aim of linguistic theory

A theory, then, in our sense of the word, may be said to aim at providing a procedural method by means of which objects of a premised nature can be described self-consistently and exhaustively. Such a self-consistent and exhaustive description 16] leads to what is usually called a knowledge or comprehension of the object in question. In a sense, then, we may also say, without risk of being misleading or obscure, that the aim of a theory is to indicate a method of procedure for knowing or comprehending a given object. But at the same time a theory is not only meant to provide us with the means of knowing one definite object. It must be so organized as to enable us to know all conceivable objects of the same premised nature as the one under consideration. A theory must be general in the sense that it must provide us with tools for comprehending not only a given object or the objects hitherto experienced, but all conceivable objects of a certain premised nature. By means of a theory we arm ourselves to meet not only the eventualities previously presented to us, but any eventuality.

The objects of interest to linguistic theory are texts. The aim of linguistic theory is to provide a procedural method by means of which a given text can be comprehended through a self-consistent and exhaustive description. But linguistic theory must also indicate how any other text of the same premised nature can be understood in the same way, and it does this by furnishing us with tools that can be used on any such text.

For example, we require of linguistic theory that it enable us to describe self-consistently and exhaustively not only a given Danish text, but also all other given Danish texts, and not only all given, but also all conceivable or possible Danish texts, including texts that will not exist until tomorrow or later, so long as they are texts of the same kind, *i.e.*, texts of the same premised nature as those heretofore considered. Linguistic theory satisfies this requirement by building on the Danish texts that have existed up to now; and since these alone are of enormous number and extent, it must be content with building on a selection from them. But by using the tools of linguistic theory, we can draw from this selection of texts a fund of knowledge to be used again on other texts. This knowledge concerns, not merely or essentially the *processes* or *texts* from which it is abstracted, but the *system* or *language* on which all texts of the same premised nature are constructed, and with the help of which we can construct new texts. With the linguistic information

17]

we have thus obtained, we shall be able to construct any conceivable or theoretically possible texts in the same language.

But linguistic theory must be of use for describing and predicting not only any possible text composed in a certain language, but, on the basis of the information that it gives about language in general, any possible text composed in any language whatsoever. The linguistic theoretician must of course attempt to satisfy this requirement likewise, by starting with a certain selection of texts in different languages. Obviously, it would be humanly impossible to work through all existing texts, and, moreover, the labor would be futile since the theory must also cover texts as yet unrealized. Hence the linguistic theoretician, like any other theoretician, must take the precaution to foresee all conceivable possibilities—even such possibilities as he himself has not experienced or seen realized—and to admit them into his theory so that it will be applicable even to texts and languages that have not appeared in his practice, or to languages that have perhaps never been realized, and some of which will probably never be realized. Only thus can he produce a linguistic theory of ensured applicability.

It is therefore necessary to ensure the applicability of the theory, and any application necessarily presupposes the theory. But it is of the greatest importance not to confuse the theory with its applications or with the practical method (procedure) of application. The theory will lead to a procedure, but no (practical) "discovery procedure" will be set forth in the present book, which does not, strictly speaking, even offer the theory in systematic form, but only its prolegomena.

By virtue of its appropriateness the work of linguistic theory is empirical, and by virtue of its arbitrariness it is calculative. From certain experiences, which must necessarily be limited even though they should be as varied as possible, the linguistic theoretician sets up a calculation of all the conceivable possibilities within certain frames. These frames he constructs arbitrarily: he discovers certain properties present in all those objects that people agree to call languages, in order then to generalize those properties and establish them by definition. From that moment the linguistic theoretician has—arbitrarily, but appropriately—himself decreed to which objects his theory can and cannot be applied. He then sets up, for all objects of the nature premised in the definition, a general calculus, in which all conceivable cases are foreseen. This calculus, which is deduced from the established definition independently of all experience, provides the tools for describing or comprehending a given text and

18] the language on which it is constructed. Linguistic theory cannot be verified (confirmed or invalidated) by reference to such existing texts and languages. It can be judged only with reference to the self-consistency and exhaustiveness of its calculus.

If, through this general calculation, linguistic theory ends by constructing several possible methods of procedure, all of which can provide a self-consistent and exhaustive description of any given text and thereby of any language whatsoever, then, among those possible methods of procedure, that one shall be chosen that results in the simplest possible description. If several methods yield equally simple descriptions, that one is to be chosen that leads to the result through the simplest procedure. This principle, which is deduced from our so-called empirical principle, we call the *simplicity principle*.

It is by reference to this principle, and only by reference to it, that we can attach any meaning to an assertion that one self-consistent and exhaustive solution is correct and another incorrect. That solution is considered the correct one which complies in the highest degree with the simplicity principle.

We may then judge linguistic theory and its applications by testing whether the solution it produces, while satisfying the requirements of self-consistency and exhaustive description, is also the simplest possible.

It is, then, by its own "empirical principle" and by it alone that linguistic theory must be tested. Consequently, it is possible to imagine several linguistic theories, in the sense of "approximations to the ideal set up and formulated in the 'empirical principle.'" One of these must necessarily be the definitive one, and any concretely developed linguistic theory hopes to be precisely that definitive one. But it follows that linguistic theory as a discipline is not defined by its concrete shape, and it is both possible and desirable for linguistic theory to progress by providing new concrete developments that yield an ever closer approximation to the basic principle.

In the prolegomena to the theory, it is in the realistic side of the theory that we shall be interested—in the best way of meeting the requirement of applicability. This will be studied by an investigation of each feature that may be said to be constitutive in the structure of any language, and by an investigation of the logical consequences of fixing those features with the aid of definitions.

19]

## 7. Perspectives of linguistic theory

Avoiding the hitherto dominant transcendent point of view and seeking an immanent understanding of language as a self-subsistent, specific structure (p. 6), and seeking a constancy within language itself, not outside it (p. 8), linguistic theory begins by circumscribing the scope of its object. This circumscription is necessary, but it is only a temporary measure and involves no reduction of the field of vision, no elimination of essential factors in the global totality which language is. It involves only a division of difficulties and a progress of thought from the simple to the complex, in conformity with Descartes' second and third rules. It is a simple consequence of the need to distinguish in order to compare, and of the indispensable principle of analysis (p. 12).

The circumscription can be considered as justified if it later permits an exhaustive and self-consistent broadening of perspective through a projection of the discovered structure on the phenomena surounding it, so that they are satisfactorily explained in the light of the structure; that is to say, if, after analysis, the global totality—language in life and actuality—may again be viewed synthetically as a whole, this time not as an accidental or merely *de facto* conglomerate, but as organized around a leading principle. In the measure that this succeeds, linguistic theory may be designated as successful. The test consists in investigating the extent to which linguistic theory satisfies the empirical principle in its requirement of an exhaustive description. The test may be made by drawing all possible general consequences from the chosen structural principle.

Linguistic theory thus makes possible a widening of perspective. How this is done *in concreto* will depend on what kind of objects we aim at first in our considerations. We choose to take our start from the premisses of previous linguistic investigation and to consider so-called *"natural" language*, and this alone, as point of departure for a linguistic theory. From this first perspective circles will be extended until the very last consequences seem to have been drawn. We shall then have to do with 20] further widenings of perspective, through which those sides of the global totality of human speech which were excluded from first consideration are again introduced and resume their place in a new whole.

### 8. *The system of definitions*

Linguistic theory, whose main task is to make explicit the specific premisses of linguistics as far back as possible, sets up for that purpose a system of definitions. It should be required of linguistic theory that it be as unmetaphysical as possible—that is to say, it must contain as few implicit premisses as possible. Its concepts must therefore be defined, and, as far as possible, the definitions must rest on defined concepts. The aim is thus in practice to define as much as possible and to introduce premised definitions before those that premise them.

It is expedient to give a strictly *formal* and at the same time explicit character to definitions that thus premise, and are premised by, other definitions. They differ from the *real* definitions for which linguistics has hitherto striven insofar as it has striven for definitions at all. In the formal definitions of the theory it is not a question of trying to exhaust the intensional nature of the objects or even of delimiting them extensionally on all sides, but only of anchoring them relatively in respect to other objects, similarly defined or premised as basic.

In certain instances it is necessary, in the course of linguistic description, to introduce, in addition to the formal definitions, *operative* definitions, whose role is only temporary. Under this term are included both such definitions as in a later stage of the procedure may be transformed into formal definitions, and purely operative definitions, whose definienda do not enter into the system of formal definitions.

This extensive defining seems to be a contributory cause of the freedom of linguistic theory from specific axioms (p. 15). As a matter of fact, it seems to us that an appropriate strategy of definition in any science will be a suitable means for lowering the number of such axioms or, in certain cases, for reducing it to zero. A purposeful attempt to eliminate implicit premises leads to replacing postulates partly by definitions and partly 21] by conditional propositions, so that the postulates as such are removed from the apparatus. Thus it seems possible in most instances to replace pure existence postulates by theorems in the form of conditions.

## 9. *Principle of the analysis*

Since linguistic theory starts from the text as its datum and attempts to show the way to a self-consistent and exhaustive description of it through an analysis—a deductive progression from class to component and component of component (pp. 12, 16) —the deepest strata of its definition system (p. 20) must treat this principle of analysis. They must establish the nature of the analysis and the concepts that enter into it. These deepest strata of the definition system will also be the very first we meet when we begin to consider what mode of progress linguistic theory must choose in order to carry out its task.

From considerations of appropriateness (*i.e.*, from consideration of the three requirements entering into the empirical principle) the choice of basis of analysis may differ for different texts. Therefore it cannot be established as universal, but only through a general calculus that takes into consideration the conceivable possibilities. What *is* universal, however, is the very principle of analysis itself, in which alone we are interested for the moment.

This too must be set up under the guidance of the empirical principle, and here it is especially the requirement of exhaustive description that has practical interest. We must consider what is necessary to ensure that the result of the analysis will be exhaustive (in a vague, preliminary sense of the term) and that we do not introduce beforehand a method that prevents us from registering factors which another analysis would reveal as also belonging to the object investigated by linguistics. We can express this by saying that the principle of analysis shall be adequate.

Naive realism would probably suppose that analysis consisted merely in dividing a given object into parts, *i.e.*, into other objects, then those again into parts, *i.e.*, into still other objects, and so on. But even naive realism would be faced with the choice between several possible ways of dividing. It soon becomes apparent that the important thing is not the division of an object into parts, but the conduct of the analysis so that 22]    it conforms to the mutual dependences between these parts, and permits us to give an adequate account of them. In this way alone the analysis becomes adequate and, from the point of view of a metaphysical theory of knowledge, can be said to reflect the "nature" of the object and its parts.

When we draw the full consequences from this, we reach a conclusion which is most important for an understanding of the principle of analysis: both the object under examination and its parts have existence only by virtue of these dependences; the whole of the object under examination can be defined only by their sum total; and each of its parts can be defined only by the dependences joining it to other coordinated parts, to the whole, and to its parts of the next degree, and by the sum of the dependences that these parts of the next degree contract with each other. After we have recognized this, the "objects" of naive realism are, from our point of view, nothing but intersections of bundles of such dependences. That is to say, objects can be described only with their help and can be defined and grasped scientifically only in this way. The dependences, which naive realism regards as secondary, presupposing the objects, become from this point of view primary, presupposed by their intersections.

The recognition of this fact, that a totality does not consist of things but of relationships, and that not substance but only its internal and external relationships have scientific existence, is not, of course, new in science, but may be new in linguistic science. The postulation of objects as something different from the terms of relationships is a superfluous axiom and consequently a metaphysical hypothesis from which linguistic science will have to be freed.

To be sure, in recent linguistic science we are to some extent attaining certain insights which, if they are thought through, must necessarily lead to this conception. Since Ferdinand de Saussure it has often been asserted that there is an interdependence between certain elements within a language, such that a language cannot have one of those elements without also having the other. The idea is doubtless correct, even if it has often been exaggerated and incorrectly applied. Everything points to the fact that Saussure, who sought *"rapports"* everywhere and asserted that a language is a form, not a substance, recognized the priority of dependences within language.

23]      At this stage of our investigation we must guard against a circular movement. If we assert, for example, that substantive and adjective, or vowel and consonant, presuppose each other, so that a language cannot have substantives without also having adjectives and *vice versa*, and cannot have vowels without also having consonants and *vice versa*—propositions that we personally think it possible to establish as theorems—then these propositions will be true or false depending on the definitions chosen for the concepts "substantive," "adjective," "vowel," "consonant."

We thus find ourselves at this stage in difficult territory. But the difficulties are increased by the fact that our examples, which we have hitherto chiefly sought in such mutual dependences or interdependences, are taken from the system of language, not from its process (p. 9) and by the fact that it is precisely this kind of dependences, and not others, that have been sought. In addition to interdependences, we must foresee unilateral dependences, where the one term presupposes the other but not *vice versa*, and further, freer dependences that consist in two terms' not entering into any relationship of presupposition but still being compatible (in the process or in the system), and thus differing from still another set of terms, those that are incompatible.

As soon as we have perceived the existence of these different possibilities, the practical demand for an appropriate terminology becomes urgent. We shall provisionally introduce terms for the possibilities we have here reckoned with. The mutual dependences, in which the one term presupposes the other and *vice versa*, we shall call conventionally *interdependences*. The unilateral dependences, in which the one term presupposes the other but not *vice versa*, we call *determinations*. And the freer dependences, in which two terms are compatible but neither presupposes the other, we call *constellations*.

To these we add the special designations for all three such dependences as they enter into a process or into a system. Interdependence between terms in a process we call *solidarity*, interdependence between terms in a system we call *complementarity*.[3]

Determination between terms in a process we call *selection*,
24] and determination between terms in a system, *specification*. Constellations within a process we call *combinations*,
and constellations within a system, *autonomies*.

It is practical to have thus at our disposal three sets of terms:
one set for use when we are speaking about a process, another
set for use when we are speaking about a system, and, finally, a
third set that can be used indifferently for both processes and
systems. The fact is that some cases are found where one and
the same collection of terms may be viewed as a process and as a
system, and where, therefore, the difference between process and
system is only a difference in point of view. The theory itself is an
example: the hierarchy of the definitions can be viewed as a
process, since first one definition is stated, written, or read, then
another, and so on; or it may be viewed as a system, that is,
as potentially underlying a possible process. The functions between the definitions are determinations, since the definitions
designed to be placed early in the process (or system) of definitions are presupposed by those designed to follow later, but not
*vice versa*. If the hierarchy of definitions is viewed as a process,
there is selection between the definitions; if it is viewed as a
system, there is specification between the definitions.

For our present investigation, which is concerned with textual
analysis, it is the process and not the system that is of interest.
If we look for solidarities within texts of an individual language,
we find them easily. For example, in a language of familiar
structure, there is very often solidarity between morphemes[4] of
different categories within a "grammatical form," such that a
morpheme of one category within such a grammatical form is

---

[3] Examples of complementarities, then, will be the relationship between substantive and adjective and the relationship between vowel and consonant.

[4] Throughout this book the term *morphemes* is restricted to use in the sense of
inflexional elements, considered as elements of the content.

necessarily accompanied by a morpheme of the other category and *vice versa*. Thus both a case morpheme and a number morpheme always enter into a Latin noun, never one of them alone. More conspicuous, however, are the selections. Some of these have long been known under the name of government, although that concept remains undefined. Between a preposition and its object there can be selection, as, for example, between Latin *sine* and the ablative, since *sine* presupposes the coexistence in the text of an ablative but not *vice versa*. In other instances there will be combination, as, for example, between Latin *ab* and the ablative, which have possible but not necessary coexistence. By having possible coexistence they differ from *ad* and the ablative, for example, which are incompatible. That *ab* and the ablative do not have necessary coexistence is concluded from the fact that *ab* can also function as a preverb. From another point of view, which is not connected with the texts of an individual language but is universal, there may be a solidarity between a preposition and its object, in the sense that the object of a preposition cannot exist without a preposition, nor a preposition (like *sine*) without an object.

25]

Conventional linguistics has been systematically interested in such dependences within the text only insofar as they occurred between two or more different words, not within one and the same word. This is bound up with the division into morphology and syntax, the necessity of which has been insisted on by conventional linguistics ever since antiquity, and which we shall shortly be led to abandon as inadequate—this time, incidentally, in agreement with several modern schools. The logical consequence of maintaining this distinction must be—and some scholars have been willing to accept this consequence—that morphology lends itself only to a description of systems and syntax only to a description of processes. It is profitable to draw these consequences, because they make the paradox immediately obvious. Logically, then, it would be possible for process dependences to be registered only within syntax, not within logology—*i.e.*, between the words of a sentence, but not within the individual word or between its parts. Hence the preoccupation with grammatical government.

But it is easy to see, even in terms of familiar concepts, that there are within the word dependences completely analogous to those of the sentence and susceptible, *mutatis mutandis*, of the same kind of analysis and description. The structure of a language may be such that a word-stem can appear both with and without derivational elements. Under this condition, there is then selection between the derivational element and the stem. From a more universal or general point of view there is always selection, in that a derivational element necessarily presupposes a stem but not *vice versa*. The terms of conventional linguistics (morphology) are thus, in the last resort, inevitably based on se-

26]     lection, just like, for example, the terms "primary clause" and "secondary clause." We have already given an example showing that within the ending of a word and between its components there are also dependences of the kinds we have described. For it is immediately apparent that, under certain structural conditions, the solidarity between the nominal morphemes may be replaced by a selection or by a combination. A noun can, for example, have or not have comparison, so that the morphemes of comparison are thus not in solidarity with, for example, the case morphemes, as are the morphemes of number, but unilaterally presuppose their coexistence; here, then, there is selection. Combination emerges, as soon as we consider, for example, each case and number separately, instead of studying, as we did above, the relationship between the whole case paradigm and the whole number paradigm: between the individual case, *e.g.*, accusative, and the individual number, *e.g.*, plural, there is combination; only between the paradigms considered *en bloc* is there solidarity. A syllable may be divided on the same principle: under certain structural conditions, which are very common, it is possible to distinguish between a central part of the syllable (the vowel, or sonant) and a marginal part (the consonant, or non-sonant) by virtue of the fact that a marginal part presupposes textual coexistence of a central part but not

*vice versa;* thus, here again there is selection. This principle is, indeed, the basis of a definition of vowel and consonant long forgotten by the pundits but still, I believe, maintained in elementary schools and undoubtedly inherited from antiquity.

It may be taken for granted that a text and any of its parts can be analyzed into parts defined by dependences of the sort discussed. The principle of analysis must, consequently, be a recognition of these dependences. It must be possible to conceive of the parts to which the analysis shall lead as nothing but intersection points of bundles of lines of dependence. Thus analysis cannot be undertaken before these lines of dependence are described in their main types, since the basis of analysis in the individual case must be chosen according to what lines of dependence are relevant—that is to say, what lines of dependence must be described to make the description exhaustive.

### 10. Form of the analysis

The analysis thus consists actually in registering certain
27]   dependences between certain terminals, which we may
call, in accordance with established usage, the parts of the text, and which have existence precisely by virtue of these dependences and only by virtue of them. The fact that we can call these terminals parts, and this whole procedure a division, or analysis, rests on the fact that we also find dependences of a particular kind between these terminals and the whole (the text) into which they are said to enter, dependences which it is then likewise the task of the analysis to register. The peculiar factor that characterizes the dependence between the whole and the parts, that makes it different from a dependence between the whole and other wholes, and that makes it possible to view the discovered objects (parts) as lying within and not outside the whole (the text), seems to be the *uniformity* of the dependence: coordinate parts, which proceed from an individual analysis of a whole, depend in a uniform fashion on that whole. This feature of uniformity we find again in the dependence between the so-

called parts. If, for example, our analysis of a text produces, at some stage, clauses and if we find two kinds of clauses (defined by a specific dependence between them)—primary clauses and secondary clauses—we shall (so long as no further analysis is undertaken) always find the same dependence between a primary clause and a secondary clause dependent on it, wherever they may appear; likewise between stem and derivational element or between the central and marginal parts of a syllable, and correspondingly in all other cases.

We shall make use of this criterion in the definition that aims at establishing and maintaining analysis in a methodologically unambiguous way. *Analysis* we can then define formally as description of an object by the uniform dependences of other objects on it and on each other. The object that is subjected to analysis we shall call a *class*, and the other objects, which are registered by a particular analysis as uniformly dependent on the class and on each other, we shall call *components* of the class.

In this first small sample of the definition system of linguistic theory, the definition of component presupposes the definition of class, and the definition of class the definition of analysis. The definition of analysis presupposes only such terms or concepts as are not defined in the specific definition system of linguistic theory, but which we posit as indefinables: *description, object, dependence, uniformity*.

28]     A class of classes we shall call a *hierarchy*, and we know that we need to distinguish between two sorts of hierarchies: *processes* and *systems*. We shall be able to approach nearer to customary and established usage by introducing separate designations for class and component respectively within a process and within a system. Classes within a linguistic[5] process we call *chains*, and components of a chain we call its *parts*. Classes within a linguistic system we call *paradigms*, and com-

----

[5] In the final, and more general, form of these two definitions, the word *linguistic* will be replaced by *semiotic*. For the distinction between a language and a semiotic, see pp. 106–110.

ponents of a paradigm we call its *members*. Corresponding to the distinction between *parts* and *members*, we shall, when it is appropriate to specify, be able to call an analysis of a process a *partition*, and an analysis of a system an *articulation*.

The first task of the analysis is, then, to undertake a partition of the textual process. The text is a chain, and all the parts (*e.g.*, clauses, words, syllables, and so on) are likewise chains, except such eventual ultimate parts as cannot be subjected to analysis.

The requirement of an exhaustive description will make it impossible to stop with a particular partition of the text; the parts that have appeared from such a partition must be again partitioned, and so on until the partition is exhausted. We have defined analysis in such a way as not to involve the question of whether it is simple or continued; an analysis (and thus also a partition), as so defined, may contain one, two, or more, analyses. Analysis, or partition, is an "accordion concept." Furthermore it can now be considered that the description of the given object (text) is not exhausted by such a continued (and in itself exhausted) partition from one basis of analysis, but that the description can be continued (*i.e.*, new dependences can be registered) through other partitions from other bases of analysis. In such instances we shall speak of an *analysis complex* (*partition complex*), *i.e.*, a class of analyses (partitions) of one and the same class (chain).

The whole textual analysis will thus take the form of a procedure, consisting of a continued partition or a partition complex, in which a single operation consists of a single minimal partition. Within this procedure each operation will premise the preceding operations and be premised by the following operations. Likewise, if the procedure is a partition complex, each of the exhausted partitions that enter therein will be premised by and/or premise other exhausted partitions 29] entering therein. Between the components of the procedure there is determination, such that the succeeding components always premise the preceding but not *vice versa:* just like the determination between the definitions (p. 25), so also the determination between the operations can be viewed as a selection or as a specification. Such a procedural whole we shall call a *deduction*, and we formally define a deduction as a continued analysis or an analysis complex with determination between the analyses that enter therein.

A deduction is thus one special kind of procedure, while induction is another special kind of procedure. Let us define an *operation* as a description that is in agreement with the empirical principle, and a *procedure* as a class of operations with mutual determination. By these definitions, both *operation* and *procedure* are "accordion concepts" (like *analysis*, above). A procedure can, then, among other things, either consist of analyses and be a deduction, or, on the other hand, consist of *syntheses* and be an *induction*. By a *synthesis* we understand a description of an object as a component of a class (and *synthesis* is then also an "accordion concept," like its opposite, *analysis*), and by an *induction* we shall understand a continued synthesis with determination between the syntheses that enter therein. If a procedure consists of both an analysis and a synthesis, the relationship between the analysis and the synthesis will always be a determination, in which the synthesis premises the analysis but not *vice versa;* this is a simple consequence of the fact that the immediate datum is the unanalyzed whole (*e.g.*, the text, *cf.* p. 12). From this it further follows that a purely inductive procedure (necessarily with implicit deduction) could not satisfy the empirical principle in its requirement of an exhaustive description. Thus a formal motivation is given for the deductive method posited in section 4. The deductive method does not, for that matter, prevent the hierarchy from being afterwards traversed in the opposite direction. No new results will be gained, but only a new point of view which it may sometimes be appropriate to adopt for the same resultants.

We have not found any real reason at this point for changing a terminology which is gaining ground in linguistics. The formal

foundation of terms and concepts given here should
30]     make possible a bridge to the established usage of episte-
        mology. Nothing is involved in the given definitions that
contradicts or makes impossible the use of the word *deduction*
in the sense of "logical conclusion." Propositions that follow
from other propositions can in our sense be said to proceed from
them by an analysis:[6] conclusions are at each step objects that
depend uniformly on each other and on the premises. It is true
that this conflicts with usual ideas about the concept of analysis;
but it is precisely by using formal definitions that we have hoped
to guard ourself against any postulates about the essence of an
object, and we have therefore not postulated anything about the
essence or nature of analysis beyond what lies in the definition.
—If *induction* is used to denote a special kind of logical argu-
ment from certain propositions to others, thus denoting, in logical terminology, a kind of deduction, then the ambiguous word
*induction* is being applied in a quite different meaning from the
one intended by us; the process of defining that we have carried
out should prevent this ambiguity from disturbing the reader.

Up to now we have used *component, part,* and *member* as con-
trasts respectively to *class, chain,* and *paradigm*. But we shall
use *component, part,* and *member* only to designate the resultants
of an individual analysis (see the definition of *component,* above);
in the case of a continued analysis we shall speak of *derivates*. A
hierarchy is then a class with its derivates. Let us imagine a
textual analysis yielding, at a certain stage, groups of syllables,
which are then analyzed into syllables, which, in turn, are analyzed into parts of syllables. In such an instance the syllables
will be derivates of the groups of syllables, and the parts of syllables will be derivates of both the groups of syllables and the
syllables. On the other hand, the parts of syllables will be components (parts) of the syllables but not of the groups of syllables,
and the syllables will be components (parts) of the groups of
syllables but of no other resultants of the analysis. Transformed

---

[6] We shall return to this subject in section 18.

into definitions: by the *derivates* of a class we shall understand its components and components-of-components within one and the same deduction; we add to this that the class is said to *include* its derivates, and the derivates to *enter into* their class. By the *degree* of the derivates we shall be referring to the number of the classes through which they are dependent on their lowest common class. If this number is 0, the derivates are said 31] to be of the 1st degree; if the number is 1, the derivates are said to be of the 2nd degree; and so forth. In the example we have constructed above, where groups of syllables are thought of as analyzed into syllables, and these into parts of syllables, the syllables will thus be first-degree derivates of the groups of syllables, while the parts of syllables will be first-degree derivates of the syllables and second-degree derivates of the groups of syllables. *First-degree derivate* and *component* are consequently equivalent terms.

## *11. Functions*

A dependence that fulfils the conditions for an analysis we shall call a *function*. Thus we say that there is a function between a class and its components (a chain and its parts, or a paradigm and its members) and between the components (parts or members) mutually. The terminals of a function we shall call its functives, understanding by a *functive* an object that has function to other objects. A functive is said to *contract* its function. From the definitions it follows that functions can be functives since there can be a function between functions. Thus there is a function between the function contracted by the parts of a chain with each other and the function contracted by the chain with its parts. A functive that is not a function we shall call an *entity*. In the example we have constructed above, the groups of syllables, the syllables, and the parts of syllables will be entities.

We have adopted the term *function* in a sense that lies midway between the logico-mathematical and the etymological sense (which latter has also played a considerable role in science, including linguistic science), in formal respect nearer to the first but not identical with it. It is precisely such an intermediate and combining concept that we need in linguistics. We shall be able to say that an entity within the text (or within the system) has certain functions, and thereby think, first of all with approximation to the logico-mathematical meaning, that the entity has dependences with other entities, such that certain entities premise others—and secondly, with approximation to the etymological meaning, that the entity functions in a definite way, fulfils a definite role, assumes a definite "position" in the chain.

32]     In a way, we can say that the etymological meaning of the word *function* is its "real" definition, which we avoid making explicit and introducing into the definition system, because it is based on more premisses than the given formal definition and turns out to be reducible to it.

By introducing the technical term *function* we seek to avoid the ambiguity that lies in the conventional use made of it in science, where it designates both the dependence between two terminals and one or both of these terminals—the latter when the one terminal is said to be "a function of" the other. The introduction of the technical term *functive* serves to avoid this ambiguity, as does the introduction of a usage that avoids saying that one functive is "a function of" the other, and replaces this with the phraseology: the one functive *has a function to* the other. The ambiguity we find here in the traditional use of the word *function* is frequently observed in the terms used to designate special kinds of functions, as when *presupposition* signifies both *postulation* and *postulate*, both a function and a functive. This ambiguous concept lies behind the "real" definitions of the kinds of functions, but precisely because of its ambiguity it is not suitable for use in their formal definitions. Still another example of this ambiguity is the word *meaning*, which denotes both designation and designatum (and which, incidentally, is unclear in other respects too).

We shall now be able to give a systematic survey of the different kinds of functions whose use we can foresee in linguistic theory and, at the same time, to give formal definitions of the functions that we have been discussing.

By a *constant* we shall understand a functive whose presence is a necessary condition for the presence of the functive to which it has function; by a *variable* we shall understand a functive whose presence is not a necessary condition for the presence of the functive to which it has function. These definitions presuppose certain non-specific indefinables (*presence, necessity, condition*) and the definitions of function and of functive.

On this basis we can define *interdependence* as a function between two constants, *determination* as a function between a constant and a variable, and *constellation* as a function between two variables.

33]    In certain instances it will be useful for us to have a common name for interdependence and determination (the two functions among whose functives appear one or more constants): we call them both *cohesions*. Likewise in certain instances we can make use of a common designation for interdependence and constellation (the two functions with the common feature that each of them has functives of one and only one kind: interdependences having only constants, constellations only variables): we call them both *reciprocities*, a name that suggests itself naturally because these two functions, in contradistinction to determination, have no fixed "orientation."

On the basis of the fixed orientation of a determination (*i.e.*, on the basis of the distinctiveness of its functives) its two functives must be named differently. The constant in a determination (selection or specification) we call the *determined (selected, specified)* functive, and the variable in a determination the *determining (selecting, specifying)* functive. The functive whose presence is a necessary condition for the presence of the other functive in the determination is said to *be determined (selected, specified) by* the latter, and the functive whose presence is not a necessary condition for the presence of the other functive in the determination is said to *determine* (*select, specify*) it. The functives that contract reciprocity can, on the other hand, be named alike: functives that contract interdependence (solidarity, complementarity) are naturally called *interdependent* (*solidary, complementary*), and functives that contract constellation (combination, autonomy) *constellative* (*combined, autonomous*). Functives that contract reciprocity are called *reciprocal*, and functives that contract cohesion *cohesive*.

We have formulated the definitions of the three kinds of functions so as to take care of the case where there are two and only two functives contracting them. It can be foreseen for all three kinds of functions that they may be contracted by more than two functives; but these *multilateral* functions can be considered as functions between *bilateral* functions.

Another important distinction for linguistic theory is the one between the both-and function, or "conjunction," and the either-or function, or "disjunction." This is what is behind the distinction between process and system: in the process, in the text, is present a both-and, a conjunction or coexistence between the functives entering therein; in the system is present an 34]    either-or, a disjunction or alternation between the functives entering therein.

Consider the (graphemic) example

*p e t*

*m a n*

By interchanging *p* and *m*, *e* and *a*, *t* and *n*, respectively, we obtain different words, namely, *pet, pen, pat, pan, met, men, mat, man*. These entities are chains that enter into the linguistic process (text); on the other hand, *p* and *m* together, *e* and *a* together, *t* and *n* together produce paradigms, which enter into the linguistic system. In *pet* there is conjunction, or coexistence, between *p* and *e* and *t*: we have "in fact" before our eyes *p* and *e* and *t*; in the same way there is conjunction or coexistence between *m* and *a* and *n* in *man*. But between *p* and *m* there is disjunction, or alternation: what we "in fact" have before our eyes is *either p or m;* in the same way there is disjunction, or alternation, between *t* and *n.*

In a certain sense it is said to be the same entities that enter into the linguistic process (text) and into the linguistic system: considered as component (derivate) of the word *pet,* *p* enters into a process and thus into conjunction, and considered as component (derivate) of the paradigm

$$p$$
$$m$$

*p* enters into a system and thus into disjunction. From the point of view of the process, *p* is a part; from the point of view of the system, *p* is a member. The two points of view lead to the recognition of two different objects, because the functional definition changes; but by uniting or multiplying the two different functional definitions we can take a point of view that justifies our saying that we have to deal with the "same" *p.* In a way we can say that all functives of language enter into both a process and a system, contract both conjunction, or coexistence, and disjunction, or alternation, and that their definition in the particular instance as conjuncts or disjuncts, coexistents or alternants, depends on the point of view from which they are surveyed.

35]     In linguistic theory—in contrast to previous linguistic science and in conscious reaction against it—we strive for an unambiguous terminology. But in few places does the linguistic theoretician find himself in such terminological difficulties as here. We have tentatively called the both-and function a conjunction (with reference to the terminology of logic) or a coexistence, and the either-or function a disjunction (also with reference to logical terminology) or an alternation. But it will be certainly inexpedient to retain these designations. Linguists are accustomed to understanding by a *conjunction* something quite different, and we are forced in agreement with tradition to use *conjunction* in a corresponding fashion (for a so-called "part of speech," even if we do not think it possible to define it as such). *Disjunction* has been used fairly widely in recent linguistic science as a specific kind of either-or function, and it would cause confusion and misunderstanding if we introduced the same term as a general designation of all either-or functions. *Alternation*, finally, is a deep-rooted and certainly ineradicable (moreover a convenient) linguistic name for a very specific kind of function (notably, the so-called ablaut and umlaut), which has strong associations with the either-or function and in reality is an especially complicated either-or function; it will therefore not do to introduce *alternation* as a general name for either-or functions. The term *coexistence*, it is true, has not been appropriated, but we do not recommend it because, among other reasons, a widespread linguistic usage connects it in a certain sense with co-existence between members of a paradigm.

We must therefore look for another solution, and here as elsewhere, insofar as possible, we shall try to make contact with already existing linguistic terminology. Now in modern linguistic science it has been a widespread practice to call the function between the members of a paradigm a *correlation*. This term seems then to be particularly well adapted for either-or functions. And as a serviceable designation for the both-and function we settle on the word *relation*. We shall thus adopt this word in a narrower meaning than it has in logic, where *relation* is used essentially in the same sense in which we use the word *function*. The initial difficulty that this may cause should be easily surmountable.

36]     We shall thus understand by *correlation*[7] the either-or function, and by *relation*[8] the both-and function. The functives that contract these functions we call respectively *correlates* and *relates*. And on this basis we can define a *system* as a

---

[7] Or *equivalence* (*cf*. H. J. Uldall, "On Equivalent Relations," *Travaux du Cercle linguistique de Copenhague* V, 71–76).

[8] Or *connexion*.

correlational hierarchy, and a *process* as a relational hierarchy.

Now, as we have already seen (pp. 9–10), process and system are concepts of great generality, which cannot be restricted exclusively to semiotic objects. We find convenient and traditional special designations for a semiotic process and a semiotic system respectively in the names *syntagmatic* and *paradigmatic*. When it is a question of language (in the ordinary sense of the word), which indeed alone interests us for the present, we can also use simpler designations: the process can here be called a *text*, and the system a *language*.

A process and a system that belongs to it ("lies behind it") together contract a function, which, depending on the point of view, may be conceived as a relation or as a correlation. A closer investigation of this function soon shows us that it is a determination in which the system is the constant: *the process determines the system*. The decisive point is not the superficial relationship consisting in the fact that the process is the more immediately accessible for observation, while the system must be "ordered to" the process—"discovered" behind it by means of a procedure—and so is only mediately knowable insofar as it is not presented to us on the basis of a previously performed procedure. This superficial relationship might make it seem that the process can exist without a system but not *vice versa*. But the decisive point is that the existence of a system is a necessary premiss for the existence of a process: the process comes into existence by virtue of a system's being present behind it, a system which governs and determines it in its possible development. A process is unimaginable—because it would be in an absolute and irrevocable sense inexplicable—without a system lying behind it. On the other hand, a system is not unimaginable without a process; the existence of a system does not presuppose the existence of a process. The system does not come into existence by virtue of a process's being found.

It is thus impossible to have a text without a language lying behind it. On the other hand, one can have a language without a text constructed in that language. This means that the language in question is foreseen by linguistic theory as a

37]     possible system, but that no process belonging to it is present as *realized*. The textual process is *virtual*. This remark obliges us to define *realization*.

An operation with a given result we shall call *universal* if it is asserted that the operation can be performed on any object whatsoever; its resultants we shall call *universals*. On the other hand, an operation with a given result we shall call *particular*, and its resultants *particulars*, if it is asserted that the operation can be performed on a certain object but not on any other object. On this basis we call a class *realized* if it can be taken as the object of a *particular analysis*, and *virtual* if this is not the case. We believe that we have thus attained a formal definition that guards us against metaphysical obligations, the necessary and sufficient fixing of what we mean by the word *realization*.

If there is present only a language (system) but no text (process) belonging to it, *i.e.*, a language foreseen as possible by the linguistic theoretician, but no texts naturally present or constructed by him from the system—then the linguistic theoretician can indeed consider the existence of such texts as a possibility, but cannot take them as objects for particular analysis. In this event, therefore, we say that the text is virtual. But even a purely virtual text presupposes a realized linguistic system in the sense of the definition. From a "real" point of view this is bound up with the fact that a process has a more "concrete" character than a system, and that a system has a more "closed" character than a process.

We shall conclude this section by presenting, with reference to the detailed analysis of functions that we undertook in section 9, a schematic survey of the kinds of functions that we have foreseen:[9]

---

[9] The use of the glossematic symbols for the various functions is illustrated by the following examples, in which *a* and *b* represent any terminals, *v* a variable terminal, and *c* a constant terminal: FUNCTION: $a \varphi b$; RELATION: $a \text{ R } b$; CORRELA-

| function | | relation (connexion) | correlation (equivalence) |
|---|---|---|---|
| cohesion { | determination | selection | specification |
| reciprocity { | interdependence | solidarity | complementarity |
| | constellation | combination | autonomy |

38]   *12. Signs and figuræ*

There is a peculiarity to be observed concerning the entities yielded by a deduction, a peculiarity which we can illustrate roughly by observing that it is possible for a sentence to consist of only one clause and a clause of only one word. This phenomenon is constantly turning up in the most various texts. In the Latin imperative *ī* "go!" or in the English interjection *ah* we have an entity that may be said to be at the same time a sentence, a clause, and a word. In each of these cases, also, we find a syllable that includes only one part of a syllable (central part, *cf*. p. 27). We must be careful to give proper consideration to this possibility in conducting the analysis. For this purpose we must introduce a special "rule of transference," which serves to prevent a given entity from being further analyzed at a too early stage of the procedure and which ensures that certain entities under given conditions are transferred unanalyzed from stage to stage, while entities of the same degree are subjected to analysis.

In each single partition we shall be able to make an inventory of the entities that have the same relations, *i.e.*, that can occupy the same "position" in the chain. We can, for example, make inventories of all the clauses that could be inserted in various positions; under certain conditions this might lead to an inven-

---

TION: $a \vdots b$; DETERMINATION: $v \ggg c$ or $c \lll v$; SELECTION: $v \rightarrow c$ or $c \leftarrow v$; SPECIFICATION: $v \vdash c$ or $c \dashv v$; INTERDEPENDENCE: $c \leftrightarrow c$; SOLIDARITY: $c \infty c$; COMPLEMENTARITY: $c + c$; CONSTELLATION: $v \mid v$; COMBINATION: $v - v$; AUTONOMY: $v \dagger v$. The number of terminals is not, of course, restricted to two.

tory of all primary clauses and an inventory of all secondary clauses. Likewise we can make inventories of all words, all syllables, and all parts of syllables with certain functions; under certain conditions this would lead to an inventory of all central parts of syllables. To satisfy the requirement of exhaustive description it will be necessary to make such inventories. Such a procedure will make it possible to register a special kind of function between the entities that can occupy one and the same position in the chain.

When we compare the inventories yielded at the various stages of the deduction, their size will usually turn out to decrease as the procedure goes on. If the text is unrestricted, *i.e.*, capable of being prolonged through constant addition of further parts, as will be the case for a living language taken as text, it will be possible to register an unrestricted number of sentences, 39] an unrestricted number of clauses, an unrestricted number of words. Sooner or later in the course of the deduction, however, there comes a point at which the number of the inventoried entities becomes restricted, and after which it usually falls steadily. Thus it seems certain that a language will have a restricted number of syllables, although that number will be relatively high. In the case of syllables permitting an analysis into central and marginal parts, the number of members in these classes will be lower than the number of syllables in the language. When the parts of syllables are further partitioned, we reach the entities which are conventionally called phonemes; their number is probably so small in any language that it can be written with two digits, and, in a good many languages, is very low (somewhere about twenty).

These facts, established through inductive experience in all languages hitherto observed, lie behind the invention of the alphabet. As a matter of fact, if there were no restricted inventories, linguistic theory could not hope to reach its goal, which is to make possible a simple and exhaustive description of the system behind the text. If no restricted inventory appeared however long the analysis were continued, an exhaustive description would be impossible. And the smaller the inventory at the concluding analysis, the better we can satisfy the empirical principle in its requirement of a simple description. Therefore there is a great importance for linguistic theory in making possible a refinement of the idea that lay at the basis of the invention of writing, namely the idea of furnishing the analysis that leads to entities of the least possible extension and the lowest possible number.

The two observations we have made here—that an entity can sometimes be of the same extension as an entity of another degree (instance *ī*); and that the size of the inventory decreases in the course of the procedure, beginning as unrestricted, then becoming restricted and then increasingly restricted—will be of importance for us when we come to consider language as *sign system*.

That a language is a system of signs seems *a priori* an evident and fundamental proposition, which linguistic theory will have to take into account at an early stage. Linguistic theory must be able to tell us what meaning can be attributed to this proposition, and especially to the word *sign*. For the present we shall have to be content with the vague conception bequeathed by tradition. According to this conception a "sign" (or, as we shall say, in anticipation of a terminological refinement to be 40] introduced later [p. 47], a *sign-expression*) is characterized first and foremost by being a sign *for* something else —a peculiarity that is likely to arouse our interest, since this seems to indicate that a "sign" is defined by a function. A "sign" functions, designates, denotes; a "sign," in contradistinction to a non-sign, is the bearer of a meaning.

We shall content ourself with this provisional conception and try on the basis of it to decide to what extent the proposition can be correct that a language is a system of "signs."

In its first stages, a certain tentative textual analysis might seem to give full support to this proposition. The entities commonly referred to as sentences, clauses, and words seem to fulfil the stated condition: they are bearers of meanings, thus "signs," and the inventories established by an analysis following such traditional lines would lead us to recognize a sign system behind the sign process. Here as elsewhere it will be of interest to try to carry out the analysis as far as possible, in order to test for an exhaustive and maximally simple description. Words are not the ultimate, irreducible signs, as the centering of conventional linguistics around the word might lead us to think. Words can be analyzed into parts which, like words, are themselves bearers of meaning: roots, derivational elements, inflexional elements. Some languages go further in this respect than others. The Latin ending *-ibus* cannot be resolved into signs of smaller extension, but is in itself a simple sign that bears both case meaning and number meaning; the Hungarian ending for the dative plural in a word like *magyaroknak* (from *magyar* 'Hungarian') is a composite sign consisting of one sign *-ok*, bearing plural meaning, and another sign *-nak*, bearing dative meaning. Such an analysis is not affected by the existence of languages without derivational and inflexional elements, or by the fact that even in languages that have such elements words may occur consisting of a root alone. Once we have made the general observation that an entity can sometimes be of the same extension as an entity of a higher degree, and in that case will have to be transferred unanalyzed from operation to operation, this fact can no longer cause us difficulties. The analysis has, precisely for this reason, the same general form in this as in all other cases, and can be continued until it can be considered exhausted. When, for example, the analysis of an English word like *in-act-iv-ate-s* is carried through in this way, it can be shown to contain five distinguishable entities which each bear meaning and which are consequently five signs.

41] In suggesting so far-reaching an analysis on a conventional basis, we should perhaps draw attention to the fact that the "meaning" which each such minimal entity can be said to bear must be understood as being a purely contextual meaning. None of the minimal entities, nor the roots, have such an "independent" existence that they can be assigned a lexical meaning. But from the basic point of view we have assumed—the continued analysis on the basis of functions in the text—there exist no other perceivable meanings than contextual meanings; any entity, and thus also any sign, is defined relatively, not absolutely, and only by its place in the context. From this point of view it is meaningless to distinguish between meanings that appear only in the context and meanings that might be assumed to have an independent existence, or—with the old Chinese grammarians—between "empty" and "full" words. The so-called lexical meanings in certain signs are nothing but artificially isolated contextual meanings, or artificial paraphrases of them. In absolute isolation no sign has any meaning; any sign-meaning arises in a context, by which we mean a situational context or explicit context, it matters not which, since in an unlimited or productive text (a living language) we can always transform a situational into an explicit context. Thus we must not imagine, for example, that a substantive is more meaningful than a preposition, or a word more meaningful than a derivational or inflexional ending. When comparing one entity with another we may speak not merely of a difference in meaning but also of different kinds of meaning, but concerning all such entities we may speak of meaning with precisely the same relative right. This is not changed by the fact that meaning in the traditional sense is a vague concept that we shall not retain in the long run without closer analysis.

But when we attempt to analyze sign-expressions in the manner suggested, inductive experience shows that in all hitherto observed languages there comes a stage in the analysis of the expression when the entities yielded can no longer be said to be bearers of meaning and thus no longer are sign-expressions. Syllables and phonemes are not sign-expressions, but only parts of sign-expressions. That a sign-expression, for example a word or an ending, can consist of one syllable and can consist of one phoneme does not mean that the syllable is a sign-expression or that the phoneme is a sign-expression. From one point of view the *s* in *in-act-iv-ate-s* is a sign-expression, from another point of view a phoneme. The two points of view lead to the recognition of two different objects. We can very well preserve the formulation that the sign-expression *s* includes one, and only one, phoneme, but this is not the same as identifying the sign-expression with that phoneme; the phoneme enters into other combinations where it is not a sign-expression (*e.g.*, in the word *sell*).

Such considerations lead us to abandon the attempt to analyze into "signs," and we are led to recognize that a description in accordance with our principles must analyze content and expression separately, with each of the two analyses eventually yielding a restricted number of entities, which are not necessarily susceptible of one-to-one matching with entities in the opposite plane.

42]

43]     The relative economy between inventory lists for signs and for non-signs corresponds entirely to what is presumably the aim of language. A language is by its aim first and foremost a sign system; in order to be fully adequate it must always be ready to form new signs, new words or new roots. But, with all its limitless abundance, in order to be fully adequate, a language must likewise be easy to manage, practical in acquisition and use. Under the requirement of an unrestricted number of signs, this can be achieved by all the signs' being constructed of non-signs whose number is restricted, and, preferably, severely restricted. Such non-signs as enter into a sign system as parts of signs we shall here call *figuræ;* this is a purely operative term, introduced simply for convenience. Thus, a language is so ordered that with the help of a handful of figuræ and through ever new arrangements of them a legion of signs can be constructed. If a language were not so ordered it would be a tool unusable for its purpose. We thus have every reason to suppose that in this feature—the construction of the sign from a restricted number of figuræ—we have found an essential basic feature in the structure of any language.

Languages, then, cannot be described as pure sign systems. By the aim usually attributed to them they are first and foremost sign systems; but by their internal structure they are first and foremost something different, namely systems of figuræ that can be used to construct signs. The definition of a language as a sign system has thus shown itself, on closer analysis, to be unsatisfactory. It concerns only the external functions of a language, its relation to the non-linguistic factors that surround it, but not its proper, internal functions.

44]

## 13. Expression and content

Up to this point we have intentionally adhered to the old tradition according to which a sign is first and foremost a sign *for* something. In this we are certainly in agreement with the popular conception and, moreover, with a conception widely held by epistemologists and logicians. But it remains for us to show that their conception is linguistically untenable, and here we are in agreement with recent linguistic thinking.

While, according to the first view, the sign is an *expression* that points to a *content* outside the sign itself, according to the second view (which is put forth in particular by Saussure and, following him, by Weisgerber[10]) the sign is an entity generated by the connexion between an expression and a content.

Which of these views shall be preferred is a question of appropriateness. In order to answer this question we shall for the moment avoid speaking about signs, which are precisely what we shall attempt to define. Instead, we shall speak of something whose existence we think we have established, namely the *sign function*, posited between two entities, an *expression* and a *con-*

[10] Leo Weisgerber, *Germanisch-romanische Monatsschrift* XV, 1927, pp. 161 ff.; *id., Indogermanische Forschungen* XXXXVI, 1928, pp. 310 ff.; *id., Muttersprache und Geistesbildung*, Göttingen, 1929.

*tent.* On this basis we shall be able to determine whether it is appropriate to consider the sign function as an external or an internal function of the entity that we shall call a *sign*.

We have here introduced *expression* and *content* as designations of the functives that contract the function in question, the sign function. This is a purely operative definition and a formal one in the sense that, in this context, no other meaning shall be attached to the terms *expression* and *content*.

There will always be solidarity between a function and (the class of) its functives: a function is inconceivable without its terminals, and the terminals are only end points for the function and are thus inconceivable without it. If one and the same entity contracts different functions in turn, and thus might apparently be said to be selected by them, it is a matter, in each case, not of one and the same functive, but of different functives, different objects, depending on the point of view that is assumed, *i.e.*, depending on the function from which the view is taken. This does not prevent us from speaking of the "same" entity from other points of view, for example from a consideration of the functions that enter into it (are contracted by its components) and establish it. If several sets of functives contract one and the same function, this means that there is solidarity between the function and the whole class of these functives, and that consequently each individual functive selects the function.

Thus there is also solidarity between the sign function and its two functives, expression and content. There will never be a sign function without the simultaneous presence of both these functives; and an expression and its content, or a content and its expression, will never appear together without the sign function's also being present between them.

The sign function is in itself a solidarity. Expression and content are solidary—they necessarily presuppose each other. An expression is expression only by virtue of being an expression of a content, and a content is content only by virtue of being a

45]

content of an expression. Therefore—except by an artificial isolation—there can be no content without an expression, or expressionless content; neither can there be an expression without a content, or content-less expression. If we think without speaking, the thought is not a linguistic content and not a functive for a sign function. If we speak without thinking, and in the form of series of sounds to which no content can be attached by any listener, such speech is an abracadabra, not a linguistic expression and not a functive for a sign function. Of course, lack of content must not be confused with lack of meaning: an expression may very well have a content which from some point of view (for example, that of normative logic or physicalism) may be characterized as meaningless, but it is a content.

If in analyzing the text we omitted to take the sign function into consideration, we should be unable to delimit the signs from each other, and we should simply be unable to provide an exhaustive (and therefore, in our sense of the word, empirical) description of the text accounting for the functions that
46] establish it (p. 22). We should simply be deprived of an objective criterion capable of yielding a useful basis of analysis.

Saussure, in order to clarify the sign function, undertook the device of trying to consider expression and content each alone, without consideration of the sign function, and reached the following result:

"Prise en elle-même, la pensée est comme une nébuleuse où rien n'est nécessairement délimité. Il n'y a pas d'idées préétablies, et rien n'est distinct avant l'apparition de la langue. ... La substance phonique n'est pas plus fixe ni plus rigide; ce n'est pas un moule dont la pensée doive nécessairement épouser les formes, mais une matière plastique qui se divise à son tour en parties distinctes pour fournir les signifiants dont la pensée a besoin. Nous pouvons donc représenter . . . la langue . . . comme une série de subdivisions contiguës dessinées à la fois sur le plan indéfini des idées confuses . . . et sur celui non moins indéterminé des sons . . . la langue élabore ses unités en se constituant entre deux masses amorphes . . . *cette combinaison produit une forme, non une substance.*"[11]

But this pedagogical *Gedankenexperiment,* however excellently carried out, is actually meaningless, and Saussure himself must have found it so. In a science that avoids unnecessary postulates there is no basis for the assumption that content-substance (thought) or expression-substance (sound-chain) precede language in time or hierarchical order, or *vice versa.* If we maintain Saussure's terminology—and precisely from his assumptions—it becomes clear that the substance depends on the form to such a degree that it lives exclusively by its favor and can in no sense be said to have independent existence.

On the other hand, it would seem to be a justifiable experiment to compare different languages and then extract, or subtract, the factor that is common to them and that remains common to all languages, however many languages are drawn into the comparison. This factor—if we exclude the structural principle that involves the sign function and all functions deducible therefrom, a principle that is naturally common *qua* principle to all languages, but one whose execution is peculiar to each individual language—this factor will be an entity defined only by its having function to the structural principle of language and to all the factors that make languages different from one another. This common factor we call *purport.*

47]        Thus we find that the chains

| | |
|---|---|
| *jeg véd det ikke* | (Danish) |
| *I do not know* | (English) |
| *je ne sais pas* | (French) |
| *en tiedä* | (Finnish) |
| *naluvara* | (Eskimo), |

despite all their differences, have a factor in common, namely the purport, the thought itself. This purport, so considered, exists provisionally as an amorphous mass, an unanalyzed entity,

---

[11] F. de Saussure, *Cours,* 2nd ed., pp. 155–157.

which is defined only by its external functions, namely its function to each of the linguistic sentences we have quoted. We may imagine this purport to be analyzed from many points of view, to be subjected to many different analyses, under which it would appear as so many different objects. It could, for example, be analyzed from one or another logical, or from one or another psychological, point of view. In each of the languages considered it has to be analyzed in a different way—a fact that can only be interpreted as indicating that the purport is ordered, articulated, formed in different ways in the different languages:

in Danish, first *jeg* ('I'), then *véd* ('know'—present indicative), then an object, *det* ('it'), then the negative, *ikke* ('not');

in English, first *I*, then a verbal concept that is not distinctly represented in the Danish sentence, then the negation, and only then the concept 'know' (but nowhere the concept corresponding to the Danish present indicative *véd*, and no object);

in French, first 'I', then a kind of negation (which is, however, completely different from the Danish and English, since it does not have the purport of a negation in all combinations), then 'know' (present indicative), and finally a peculiar special sign which some call a negative, but which can also mean 'step'; as in English, no object;

in Finnish, first a verb signifying 'I-not' (or, more precisely, 'not-I', since the sign for 'I' comes last; the negation in Finnish is a verb that is inflected in person and number: *en* 'I-not', *et* 'thou-not', *ei* 'he-not', *emme* 'we-not', *etc.*), and then the concept 'know' in the form that has imperative meaning in other combinations; no object;

in Eskimo, 'not-knowing-am-I-it', a verb derived from *nalo* 'ignorance', with the suffix for the first-person subject and third-person object.[12]

48]       We thus see that the unformed purport extractable

[12] We have disregarded the fact that the same purport can also be formed in quite different chains in some of the languages: French *je l'ignore*, Eskimo *asuk* or *asukiaᴋ* (derived from *aso*, which by itself means 'enough!').

from all these linguistic chains is formed differently in each language. Each language lays down its own boundaries within the amorphous "thought-mass" and stresses different factors in it in different arrangements, puts the centers of gravity in different places and gives them different emphases. It is like one and the same handful of sand that is formed in quite different patterns, or like the cloud in the heavens that changes shape in Hamlet's view from minute to minute. Just as the same sand can be put into different molds, and the same cloud take on ever new shapes, so also the same purport is formed or structured differently in different languages. What determines its form is solely the functions of the language, the sign function and the functions deducible therefrom. Purport remains, each time, substance for a new form, and has no possible existence except through being substance for one form or another.

We thus recognize in the linguistic *content*, in its process, a specific *form*, the *content-form*, which is independent of, and stands in arbitrary relation to, the *purport*, and forms it into a *content-substance*.

No long reflexion is needed to see that the same is true for the *system* of the content. A paradigm in one language and a corresponding paradigm in another language can be said to cover one and the same zone of purport, which, abstracted from those languages, is an unanalyzed, amorphous continuum, on which boundaries are laid by the formative action of the languages.

Behind the paradigms that are furnished in the various languages by the designations of color, we can, by subtracting the differences, disclose such an amorphous continuum, the color spectrum, on which each language arbitrarily sets its boundaries. While formations in this zone of purport are for the most part approximately the same in the most widespread European languages, we need not go far to find formations that are incongruent with them. In Welsh, 'green' is *gwyrdd* or *glas*, 'blue' is *glas*, 'gray' is *glas* or *llwyd*, 'brown' is *llwyd*. That is to say, the part of the spectrum that is covered by our word *green* is intersected in Welsh by a line that assigns a part of it to the same area as our word *blue* while the English boundary between *green* and *blue* is not found in Welsh. Moreover, Welsh lacks the English boundary between *blue* and *gray*, and likewise the English boundary between *gray* and *brown*. On the other hand, the area that is covered by English *gray* is intersected in Welsh so that half of it is referred to the same area as our *blue* and half to the same area as our *brown*. A schematic confrontation shows the lack of coincidence between the boundaries:

49]

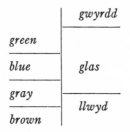

Similarly Latin and Greek show incongruence with the chief modern European languages in this sphere.—The progression from 'light' to 'dark', which is divided into three areas in English and many languages (*white, gray, black*) is divided in other languages into a different number of areas, through abolition or, on the other hand, elaboration of the middle area.

Morpheme paradigms show a similar state of affairs. The zone of number is analyzed differently in languages that distinguish only a singular and a plural, in those that add a dual (like Ancient Greek and Lithuanian), and in languages that also have a paucal—either simply a trial (like most Melanesian languages, the West Indonesian language Saŋir on the islands between Mindanao and the Celebes, and the Southeastern Australian language Kulin in some of its dialects) or also a quadral (like the Micronesian language on the Gilbert Islands). The tense zone is analyzed differently in languages which (apart from periphrastic formations) have only a preterite and a present (as, for example, English), and where therefore the present also covers

the area that is covered in other languages by the future, and
in languages that set a limit between present and future; again,
the boundaries are different in a language which (like Latin,
Ancient Greek, French) distinguishes several kinds of preterite.

50]          This incongruence within one and the same zone of purport turns up everywhere. Compare also, for example, the
following correspondences between Danish, German, and
French:

|  | *Baum* | *arbre* |
|---|---|---|
| *træ* | *Holz* | *bois* |
| *skov* | *Wald* | *forêt* |

We may conclude from this fact that in one of the two entities
that are functives of the sign function, namely the content, the
sign function institutes a form, the *content-form*, which from the
point of view of the purport is arbitrary and which can be explained only by the sign function and is obviously solidary with
it. In this sense, Saussure is clearly correct in distinguishing between form and substance.

Precisely the same thing can be observed in the other of the
two entities that are functives of the sign function, namely the
expression. Just as, for example, the color zone or the morpheme
zones are subdivided differently in different languages in that
each language has its own number of color words, its own number
of numbers, its own number of tenses, *etc.*, so we can also disclose, by subtraction from a comparison of languages, zones in
the phonetic sphere which are subdivided differently in different
languages. We can, for example, think of a phonetico-physiologi-
cal sphere of movement, which can of course be represented as
spatialized in several dimensions, and which can be presented
as an unanalyzed but analyzable continuum—for example on the
basis of Jespersen's system of "antalphabetic" formulæ. In such
an amorphous zone are arbitrarily included in different languages
a different number of figuræ (phonemes) since the boundaries are

laid down in different places within the continuum. An example is the continuum made by the median profile of the roof of the mouth, from the pharynx to the lips. In familiar languages this zone is usually divided into three areas, a back *k*-area, a middle *t*-area, and a front *p*-area. If we consider only the stops, however, Eskimo and Lettish, among others, distinguish two *k*-areas, whose lines of division do not coincide in the two languages. Eskimo places the boundary between a uvular and a velar area,

51] Lettish between a velar and a velo-palatal area. Many languages of India distinguish two *t*-areas, a retroflex and a dental; and so on. Another such obvious continuum is that of the vowel zone; the number of vowels varies from language to language, with the boundaries set differently. Eskimo distinguishes only between an *i*-area, a *u*-area, and an *a*-area. In most familiar languages the first is split into a narrower *i*-area and an *e*-area, the second into a narrower *u*-area and an *o*-area. In some languages each of these areas, or one of them, can be intersected by a line that distinguishes rounded vowels (*y*, *ø*; *u*, *o*) from unrounded (*i*, *e*; *ɯ*, *ɤ*; these last—curious "dull" vowels which are rare in Europe—or one of them, are found, for example, in Tamil, in many of the Eastern Uralic languages, and in Rumanian); with the aperture of *i* and *u* can be formed, besides, midvowels, rounded (*ʉ*) as in Norwegian and Swedish, or unrounded (*ɨ*) as in Russian; and so on. Especially because of the extraordinary mobility of the tongue, the possibilities that language can make use of are quite indefinitely great; but the characteristic thing is that each language lays down its boundaries within this infinity of possibilities.

Since the state of affairs for the expression is evidently quite analogous to that of the content, it will be appropriate for us to be able to underline this parallelism by using the same terminology for the expression as for the content. We should then be able to speak here of an *expression-purport*, and even if this is unusual there seems to be nothing beyond that fact to prevent us. The examples we have given, the vocalic continuum and the

median profile of the roof of the mouth, are then the phonetic
zones of purport, which are formed differently in different languages, depending on the specific functions of each language, and
which are thereby ordered to their expression-*form* as expression-
*substance*.

We have observed this for the *system* of expression; but just
as with the content, we can also demonstrate the same for the
*process*. Purely by virtue of the cohesion between system and
process, the specific formation of the system in a given language
inevitably involves effects in the process. Partly because of the
very boundaries that are laid in the system and that are incongruent from language to language, and partly because of the
possibilities of relation between the phonemes in the chain (some
languages, for example various Australian and African languages, admit no consonant groups at all, others only certain
definite consonant groups, different in different languages;
52]      the placing of the accent in the word is governed by different laws in different languages) *one and the same expression-purport may be formed differently* in different languages.
English [bə:ˈlɪn], German [b̥ɛrˈliːn], Danish [b̥æʁˈliˀn], Japanese
[bɛɭuɭinu] represent different formations of one and the same
expression-purport (the city-name *Berlin*). It is, of course, in-
different that the content-purport happens to be the same in
this instance; in the same way we could say that, for example,
the pronunciation of English *got*, German *Gott* ('God'), and
Danish *godt* ('well') represent different formations of one and
the same expression-purport. In this example the expression-
purport is the same, but the content-purport different, just as
in *jeg véd det ikke* and *I do not know* the content-purport is the
same but the expression-purport different.

When a person familiar with the functional system of a given
language (*e.g.*, his mother tongue) has perceived a content-
purport or an expression-purport, he will form it in that language. An essential part of what is popularly called "speaking
with an accent" consists in forming a perceived expression-

purport according to predispositions suggested by functional facts in the speaker's mother tongue.

This investigation shows us, then, that the two entities that contract the sign function—expression and content—behave in the same way in relation to it. By virtue of the sign function and only by virtue of it, exist its two functives, which can now be precisely designated as the content-form and the expression-form. And by virtue of the content-form and the expression-form, and only by virtue of them, exist respectively the content-substance and the expression-substance, which appear by the form's being projected on to the purport, just as an open net casts its shadow down on an undivided surface.

If we now return to the question from which we began, concerning the most appropriate meaning of the word *sign*, we are in a position to see more clearly behind the controversy between the traditional and the modern linguistic points of view. It seems to be true that a sign is a sign for something, and that this something in a certain sense lies outside the sign itself. Thus the word *ring* is a sign for that definite thing on my finger, and that thing does not, in a certain (traditional) sense, enter into the sign itself. But that thing on my finger is an entity of content-substance, which, through the sign, is ordered to a content-form and is arranged under it together with various other entities of content-substance (*e.g.*, the sound that comes from my telephone).

53] That a sign is a sign for something means that the content-form of a sign can subsume that something as content-substance. Just as we felt before a need to use the word *purport*, not simply of the content, but also of the expression, so here again, in the interest of clarity, despite the time-honored concepts whose shortcomings now become increasingly evident, we feel a desire to invert the sign-orientation: actually we should be able to say with precisely the same right that a sign is a sign for an expression-substance. The sound sequence [rɪŋ] itself, as a unique phenomenon, pronounced *hic et nunc*, is an entity of expression-substance which, by virtue of the sign and only by virtue thereof, is ordered to an expression-form and classified under it together with various other entities of expression-substance (other possible pronunciations, by other persons or on other occasions, of the same sign).

The sign is, then—paradoxical as it may seem—a sign for a content-substance and a sign for an expression-substance. It is in this sense that the sign can be said to be a sign for something. On the other hand, we see no justification for calling the sign a sign merely for the content-substance, or (what nobody has thought of, to be sure) merely for the expression-substance. The sign is a two-sided entity, with a Janus-like perspective in two directions, and with effect in two respects: "outwards" toward the expression-substance and "inwards" toward the content-substance.

All terminology is arbitrary, and consequently nothing prevents us from using the word *sign* as a special name for the expression-form (or, if we wished, for the expression-substance, but this would be both absurd and unnecessary). But it appears more appropriate to use the word *sign* as the name for the unit consisting of content-form and expression-form and established by the solidarity that we have called the sign function. If *sign* is used as the name for the expression alone or for a part of it, the terminology, even if protected by formal definitions, will run the risk of consciously or unconsciously giving rise to or favoring the widespread misconception according to which a language is simply a nomenclature or a stock of labels intended to be fastened on pre-existent things. The word *sign* will always, by reason of its nature, be joined to the idea of a designatum; the word *sign* must therefore be used appropriately in such a way that the relation between sign and designatum will appear as clearly as possible and not be subjected to distorting simplification.

54]    The distinction between expression and content and their interaction in the sign function is basic to the structure of any language. Any sign, any system of signs, any system of figuræ ordered to the purpose of signs, any language, contains in itself an expression-form and a content-form. The first stage of the analysis of a text must therefore be an analysis into these two entities. To be exhaustive, the analysis must be so organized that at each stage we analyze into the parts that are of greatest extension, *i.e.*, of lowest number, either within the analyzed chain in its totality or within any arbitrary section of it. If a text, for example, includes both sentences and clauses, we can show that the number of clauses is greater than the number of sentences; therefore we must not proceed directly to an analysis into clauses, but first analyze into sentences and then analyze the sentences into clauses. When this principle is carried through, it will appear that any text must always be analyzed in the first stage into two and only two parts, whose minimal number guarantees their maximal extension: namely, the *expression line* and the *content line*, which have mutual solidarity through the sign function. After that, the expression line and the content line are each analyzed further, naturally with consideration of their interaction in the signs. In the same way, the first articulation of a linguistic system will lead us to establish its two most inclusive paradigms: the *expression side* and the *content side*. As common names for *expression line* and *expression side*, on the one hand, and for *content line* and *content side*, on the other, we have used respectively the designations *expression plane* and *content plane* (designations chosen with reference to Saussure's formulation cited above: "le plan . . . des idées . . . et celui . . . des sons").

Through the whole analysis, this method of procedure proves to result in great clarity and simplification, and it also casts light on the whole mechanism of a language in a fashion hitherto unknown. From this point of view it will be easy to organize the subsidiary disciplines of linguistics according to a well-founded plan and to escape at last from the old, halting division of linguistics into phonetics, morphology, syntax, lexicography, and semantics—a division that is unsatisfactory in many respects and also involves some overlapping. But besides, when the analysis is carried through, it shows that expression plane and content plane can be described exhaustively and consistently as being structured in quite analogous fashions, so that quite identically defined categories are foreseen in the two 55] planes. This means a further essential confirmation of the correctness of conceiving expression and content as coordinate and equal entities in every respect.

The terms *expression plane* and *content plane* and, for that matter, *expression* and *content* are chosen in conformity with established notions and are quite arbitrary. Their functional definition provides no justification for calling one, and not the other, of these entities *expression*, or one, and not the other, *content*. They are defined only by their mutual solidarity, and neither of them can be identified otherwise. They are each defined only oppositively and relatively, as mutually opposed functives of one and the same function.

### 14. *Invariants and variants*

This insight into the structure of the sign is an indispensable condition for conducting the analysis precisely and, especially, for recognizing the figuræ of which a linguistic sign is composed (p. 46). At each stage of the analysis an inventory must be made of entities with uniform relations (p. 41). The inventory must satisfy our empirical principle (p. 11): it must be both exhaustive and as simple as possible. This requirement must be met at each stage, because, among other reasons, we cannot know beforehand whether any given stage is the last. But the requirement has a double importance for the concluding stage of the analysis, because there we come to recognize the ultimate entities which are basic to the system, the entities of which we must be able to demonstrate that all the other entities are constructed. And here it is important, not only for the simplicity of the solution in this last stage, but for the simplicity of the solution as a whole, that the number of these ultimate entities be as low as possible.

We formulate this requirement in two principles, the *principle*

*of economy* and the *principle of reduction,* which are both deduced
from the principle of simplicity (p. 18).

*The principle of economy: The description is made through a
procedure. The procedure shall be so arranged that the result is the
simplest possible, and shall be suspended if it does not lead to
further simplification.*

*The principle of reduction: Each operation in the procedure shall
be continued or repeated until the description is exhausted, and shall
at each stage lead to the registration of the lowest possible number
of objects.*

56]     We shall call the entities that are inventoried at each
        stage *elements.* In respect of the analysis we give the fol-
lowing *refined formulation of the principle of reduction:*

*Each analysis (or each analysis complex) in which functives are
registered with a given function as basis of analysis shall be so made
that it leads to the registration of the lowest possible number of
elements.*

In order to satisfy this requirement we must have at our disposal a method that allows us under precisely fixed conditions
to *reduce* two entities to one, or, as it is often put, to *identify*
two entities with each other.[13] If we imagine a text analyzed into
sentences, these into clauses, these into words, *etc.,* and an inventory taken for each analysis, we shall always be able to ob-

[13] In this latter formulation, the theory presupposes on this point a closer
analysis of the concept of *linguistic identity.* This has been treated from many
points of view in the recent literature (*e.g.,* by F. de Saussure, *Cours,* 2nd ed.,
pp. 150 ff., and, on the basis of Russell's hierarchy of types, by A. Penttilä (*Actes
du IVe Congrès international de linguistes,* København, 1938, pp. 160 ff.) following
U. Saarnio, *Untersuchungen zur symbolischen Logik* (*Acta philosophica Fennica* I,
Helsingfors, 1935); *cf.* Penttilä & Saarnio in *Erkenntnis* IV, 1934, pp. 28 ff.).
The provisional results thus obtained seem, however, sufficient to indicate that
this is a difficult way of arriving at the method through formal definitions, and
that we can do so more simply through the concept of *reduction.* The problem of
identity can therefore be dismissed in this connexion as an unnecessary complication.

serve that in many places in the text we have "one and the same" sentence, "one and the same" clause, "one and the same" word, *etc.:* many specimens of each sentence, each clause, each word, *etc.,* can be said to occur. These specimens we shall call *variants,* and the entities of which they are specimens, *invariants.* Moreover, it is immediately seen that not only entities, but also functions have variants, so that the distinction between variants and invariants is valid for functives in general. At each stage of the analysis we must be able to infer from variants to invariants with the help of a specially prepared method that establishes the necessary criteria for such a reduction.

Where it is a matter of highest-degree invariants of the 57] expression plane—as concerns spoken language, in theory up to this time, the so-called phonemes—in modern linguistics a certain amount of attention has been paid to this question and the first attempts have been made to work out such a method of reduction. In many instances, however, investigators have stopped at a more or less vague "real" definition of the phoneme that yields no useful objective criteria in doubtful cases. Two schools in modern linguistics have consciously sought to work out an objective method of reduction, namely the London school, as represented by Daniel Jones, and the phonological school that has its source in the Prague Circle and whose leader was N. S. Trubetzkoy. The methods of reduction worked out in these two camps display a characteristic similarity and an interesting difference.

The similarity consists in the fact that neither school recognizes that the prerequisite for an inventory is a textual analysis made on the basis of functions. The method used is the inductive one (pp. 11–12), which takes as its datum a mass of individual sounds, to be grouped into classes of sounds, the so-called phonemes. This grouping of sounds into phonemes must then, in principle, take place without consideration of what paradigms the sounds enter. With a curious inconsistency, nevertheless, both schools start with a certain rough division of the total sound-inventory of a language into categories, treating vowels and consonants separately. But vowel and consonant are regarded as categories defined, not by linguistic functions, but rather by non-linguistic (physiological or physical) premisses. And the category of vowels and the category of consonants are not analyzed at the beginning of the operation into sub-categories on the basis of relation (according to their "position" in the syllable).

In this point of similarity there is nothing surprising, since the deductive method we have outlined (p. 13) has not hitherto been practised in linguistic science.

The difference between the two schools in method of procedure, on the other hand, is of no small methodological interest. Both schools agree in seeing something characteristic in the fact that phonemes—in contrast to variants—have a *distinctive* function: the exchange of one phoneme for another can entail a difference in content (*e.g.*, *pet—pat*), while this is not possible if one variant is exchanged for another variant of the same phoneme (*e.g.*, two different pronunciations of the *e* in *pet*). The Prague phonologists set up this criterion in their definition, by defining a phonemic opposition as a distinctive opposition.[14] The

58] London school takes another way. Daniel Jones does, indeed, point out that phonemes are distinctive, but he does not wish to incorporate this feature in the definition of the phoneme, because phonemic oppositions are found that are incapable of entailing a difference in content, since the phonemes concerned cannot be exchanged for each other within one and the same word, *i.e.*, not in one and the same "position" in the chain; so, for example, *h* and *ŋ* in English.[15] This difficulty arises because Jones' theory does not recognize the fact that phonemes can

---

[14] *Actes du Ier Congrès international de linguistes*, Leiden, n.d., p. 33. *Travaux du Cercle linguistique de Prague* IV, 1931, p. 311. N. S. Trubetzkoy, *Grundzüge der Phonologie* (*Travaux du Cercle linguistique de Prague* VII, 1939), p. 30.
[15] D. Jones, *Travaux du Cercle linguistique de Prague* IV, 1931, pp. 77 f. D. Jones, *An Outline of English Phonetics*, Cambridge, 1936, pp. 49 f.

differ simply by belonging to different categories (beyond the distinction between vowel and consonant). Thus it is not considered a sufficiently distinctive criterion that *h*, which can stand only initially in a syllable, and *ŋ*, which can stand only finally in a syllable, each enter into distinctive opposition to other phonemes which can occupy the same "position" (*e.g.*, *hat—cat, sing—sit*). The London school therefore attempts to exclude the relevance of the distinctive function and instead— at least in theory—to build on the "position" of the phoneme without consideration of the distinctive function, so that two sounds that can appear in the same position are always referred to different phonemes.[16] But it is obvious that this creates new difficulties, particularly because variants, also, can appear in the same "position" (*e.g.*, *pet* with *e* of different qualities). To eliminate this difficulty it is necessary to introduce in addition to the phoneme another concept, the *variphone*, whose relation to the phoneme is not quite clear. Since any new specimen of a phoneme is necessarily a new variant, each phoneme will have variants in one and the same "position," whence it follows that each phoneme must be a *variphone*. But it appears, even if it is not expressly stated, that the different *variphones* can be considered different from each other only in their distinctive opposition.[17]

59]    The London school's attempt to avoid distinctive opposition is instructive. It was probably made in the belief that there is surer ground within pure phonetics and without appeal to the content, where the distinction between differences and similarities can be more precarious since the analytical method is less well developed in this field and objective criteria seem more difficult to obtain. Apparently the Prague Circle felt the same way, since it tries to use only what is called "differentia-

[16] D. Jones, *Le maître phonétique*, 1929, pp. 43 f., *Travaux du Cercle linguistique de Prague* IV, p. 74.

[17] D. Jones, *Proceedings of the International Congress of Phonetic Sciences* (*Archives néerlandaises de phonétique expérimentale* VIII-IX, 1933), p. 23.

tions of intellectual meaning." But the Prague Circle is undoubtedly right in holding fast to the distinctive criterion as the relevant one; the attempt of the London school shows the insuperable difficulties that otherwise appear. The strong assertion of this principle is the chief merit of the Prague Circle; on all other points strong reservations must be made concerning its theory and its practice in what it calls phonology.

Experience of previously attempted methods of reduction seems, then, to show that we must consider the distinctive factor as the relevant one for registering invariants and for distinguishing between invariants and variants. There is a difference between invariants in the expression plane when there is a correlation (*e.g.*, the correlation between *e* and *a* in *pet—pat*) to which there is a corresponding correlation in the content plane (the correlation between the content entities 'pet' and 'pat') so that we can register a *relation* between the expression-correlation and the content-correlation. This relation is an immediate consequence of the sign function, the solidarity between the form of the expression and the form of the content.

In certain methods within conventional linguistics, as we have seen, an approach to recognizing this fact has been made in modern times; it has been worked out seriously, however, only for figuræ of the expression plane. But to understand the structure of a language and to conduct the analysis, it is of the greatest importance to realize that this principle must be extended so as to be valid for all the other invariants of the language as well, irrespective of their degree or, in general, of their place in the system. The principle holds true, therefore, for all entities of expression, regardless of their extension, and not only for the minimal entities; and it is true for the content plane just as much as for the expression plane. Actually, this is only the logical consequence of recognizing the principle for the figuræ of the expression.

60]     If we consider signs instead of figuræ, and not one individual sign but two or more signs in mutual correlation, we shall always find that there is a relation between a correlation of expression and a correlation of content. If such a relation is not present, that is precisely the criterion for deciding that there are not two different signs, but only two different variants of the same sign. If the exchange of one sentence-expression for another can entail a corresponding exchange between two different sentence-contents, there are two different sentences in the expression; if not, there are two sentence variants in the expression, two different specimens of one and the same sentence-expression. The same is true for word-expressions and for any other sign-expressions. And the same is true for figuræ, regardless of their extension—syllables, for example. The difference between signs and figuræ in this respect is only that, in the case of signs, it will always be the same difference of content that is entailed by one and the same difference of expression, but in the case of figuræ, one and the same difference of expression may, in each instance, entail different changes between entities of the content (*e.g.*, *pet—pat, led—lad, ten—tan*).

Moreover the observed relation is reversible, in the sense that the distinction between invariants and variants within the content plane must be made according to exactly the same criterion (there are two different invariants of content if their correlation has relation to a correlation in the expression, otherwise not). Thus in practice there are two different invariants of content if an exchange of one for the other can entail a corresponding exchange in the expression plane. In the case of signs, this is especially and immediately obvious. If, for example, the exchange of one sentence-expression for another entails a corresponding exchange between two sentence-contents, then the exchange of one of the sentence-contents for the other will entail a corresponding exchange between the two sentence-expressions; this is only the same thing seen from the opposite side.

Finally, it is an inevitable logical consequence that this exchange test can be applied to the content plane, and not to the expression plane only, and that it must enable us to register the

figuræ that compose the sign-contents. Quite as in the expression
plane, the existence of figuræ will only be a logical conse-
61]    quence of the existence of signs. It may therefore be pre-
dicted with certainty that such an analysis can be carried
out. And it can be added at once that it is of the greatest importance that it be carried out, because such a work is a necessary
prerequisite for an exhaustive description of the content. Such
an exhaustive description presupposes the possibility of explain-
ing and describing an unlimited number of signs, in respect of
their content as well, with the aid of a limited number of figuræ.
And the reduction requirement must be the same here as for the
expression plane: the lower we can make the number of content-
figuræ, the better we can satisfy the empirical principle in its
requirement of the simplest possible description.

Till now, such an analysis into content-figuræ has never been
made or even attempted in linguistics, although a corresponding
analysis into expression-figuræ is as old as the very invention of
alphabetic writing (not to say older: after all, the invention of
alphabetic writing presupposes an attempt at such an analysis
of the expression). This inconsistency has had the most cata-
strophic consequences: confronted by an unrestricted number of
signs, the analysis of the content has appeared to be an insoluble
problem, a labor of Sisyphus, an impassable mountain.

But the method of procedure will be exactly the same for the
content plane as for the expression plane. Just as the expression
plane can, through a functional analysis, be resolved into components with mutual relations (as in the ancient discovery of
alphabetic writing and in modern phonemic theories), so also
the content plane must be resolved by such an analysis into components with mutual relations that are smaller than the minimal-
sign-contents.

Let us imagine that in the analysis of a text, at that stage of
the analysis where certain larger chains (we may think, for example, of word-expressions in a language of familiar structure) are
partitioned into syllables, the following syllables have been

registered: *sla, sli, slai, sa, si, sai, la, li, lai*. At the next stage,
where the syllables are partitioned into central (selected) and
marginal (selecting) parts (p. 27), a mechanical inventory in
the categories of central and marginal parts of syllables would
yield, respectively, *a, i, ai*, and *sl, s, l*. But since *ai* may
be explained as a unit established by the relation between
*a* and *i*, and *sl* as a unit established by the relation between *s* and *l*, *ai* and *sl* are struck out of the inventory of elements. There remain only *a* and *i, s* and *l*, so that these are also
defined by their faculty of entering the "groups" mentioned (the
consonant group *sl* and the diphthong *ai*). And it is well to note:
this reduction must be undertaken in the same operation in
which central and marginal parts of syllables are registered, and
it must not be deferred to the next operation, in which these
parts are again partitioned into smaller parts. To proceed otherwise would be to conflict both with the requirement of the simplest possible procedure and with the requirement of the simplest
possible result in any particular operation (*cf*. p. 18 and the
principle of reduction). If, however, we had another situation,
in which, on analyzing larger chains into syllables, we had found
only *slai*, but not *sla, sli, sa, si, sai, la, li, lai*—then the reduction
could not be carried further by resolution of syllables into parts,
and further reduction would have to be postponed to the following operation, in which the parts of syllables would be taken as
objects for further partition. If, to give another example, we had
*slai, sla*, and *sli*, but not *sai, sa, si, lai, la, li*, we should be able to
resolve *ai* at this stage of the procedure, but not *sl*. (If we had
*slai* and *sla*, but not *sli*, the resolution could not be undertaken,
and *ai* and *a* would have to be registered as two different invariants. Violating this rule would, among other results, lead to
the absurdity that, in a language having the syllables *a* and *sa*,
but no syllable *s*, we should register not merely *a* but also *s* as a
separate invariant in the inventory of syllables.)

In this method of procedure there is in principle a factor of
generalization. The reduction can be carried out only if it is

62]

possible to generalize from case to case without risk of inconsistency. In our example we may imagine the modification introduced that *sl* can be reduced to a group only in some cases, but not in all, because the content associated with the syllable *sla* with unresolved *sl* is different from the content associated with the syllable *sla* with resolved *sl*, whence it must follow that *sl* is an element on a line with *s* and *l*. In several well-known languages (*e.g.*, English) the entity *t∫* can be resolved into *t* and *∫*, so that this resolution may be generalized consistently to all cases. In Polish, however, *t∫* exists as an independent entity on a line with *t* and *∫*, while these latter can enter into a group

63]  *t∫* (functionally distinct from *t∫*): the two words *trzy* 'three' and *czy* 'whether' differ in pronunciation only by the first's having *t∫* and the second *t∫*.[18]

It is therefore of practical importance here to make use of a special *principle of generalization*. Moreover, the practical significance of this principle shows up at many other points within linguistic theory, and it must therefore be posited as one of the general principles of the theory. We believe it possible to prove that this principle has always implicitly played a role in scientific research, although so far as we know it has not previously been formulated. It goes as follows:

*If one object admits of a solution univocally, and another object admits of the same solution equivocally, then the solution is generalized to be valid for the equivocal object.*

The rule that applies to the reductions here discussed can accordingly be formulated as follows:

*Entities which, on application of the principle of generalization,*

---

[18] L. Bloomfield, *Language*, New York, 1933, p. 119. George L. Trager, *Acta Linguistica* I, 1939, p. 179. A thorough-going analysis of the Polish system of expression from our points of view will probably disclose further differences between the two cases; this does not, however, weaken the principle or its application at a certain stage of the analysis. Something of the sort is true of Jones' example of English *h* and *ŋ*.

*may be univocally registered as complex units including only ele-*
*ments registered in the same operation, must not be registered as*
*elements.*

This rule is then to be applied in the content plane in just the
same way as in the expression plane. If, for example, a mechanical inventorying at a given stage of the procedure leads to a
registration of the entities of content 'ram', 'ewe', 'man',
'woman', 'boy', 'girl', 'stallion', 'mare', 'sheep', 'human being',
'child', 'horse', 'he', and 'she'—then 'ram', 'ewe', 'man',
'woman', 'boy', 'girl', 'stallion', and 'mare' must be eliminated
from the inventory of elements if they can be explained univocally as relational units that include only 'he' or 'she' on the one
hand, and 'sheep', 'human being', 'child', 'horse' on the other.
Here, as in the expression plane, the criterion is the exchange
test, by which a relation is found between correlations in each of
the two planes. Just as exchanges between *sai*, *sa*, and *si*
64]     can entail exchanges between three different contents, so
exchanges between the content-entities 'ram', 'he', and
'sheep' can entail exchanges between three different expressions.
'Ram' = 'he-sheep' will be different from 'ewe' = 'she-sheep',
just as *sl* will be different from, say, *fl*, and 'ram' = 'he-sheep'
will be different from 'stallion' = 'he-horse', just as *sl* will be different from, say, *sn*. The exchange of one and only one element
for another is in both cases sufficient to entail an exchange in
the other plane of the language.

In the little examples to which we have had recourse in the
foregoing (partition of sentences into clauses, and clauses into
words; partition of groups of syllables into syllables, of these
into parts of syllables, and of these into smaller figuræ) we have,
in accord with traditional concepts, provisionally spoken as if
the text consisted only of an expression line. We have been led
in the preceding section (p. 60) to perceive that, after partition-
ing the text into expression line and content line, we must partition each of these according to a common principle. Conse-

quently, this partition must be carried out equally far (*i.e.*, to the end) in both lines. Just as with a continued partition of the expression line we sooner or later approach a boundary where unrestricted inventories are resolved into restricted, after which these restricted inventories constantly decrease in size through the further operations (p. 42), so the very same thing will occur in an analysis of the content line. The analysis into figuræ in the expression plane can be said to consist, in practice, in the resolution of entities that enter unrestricted inventories (*e.g.*, word-expressions) into entities that enter restricted inventories, and this resolution is carried on until only the most restricted inventories remain. The same will hold true of the analysis into figuræ in the content plane. While the inventory of word-contents is unrestricted, in a language of familiar structure even the minimal signs will be distributed (on the basis of relational differences) into some (selected) inventories, which are unrestricted (*e.g.*, inventories of root-contents), and other (selecting) inventories, which are restricted (*e.g.*, inventories embracing contents of derivational and inflexional elements, *i.e.*, derivatives and morphemes). Thus in practice the procedure consists in trying to analyze the entities that enter the unrestricted inventories purely into entities that enter the restricted inventories. In the example we have used above, this principle is seen to be already carried out in part: while 'sheep', 'human being', 'child', 65] and 'horse' remain for the present in unrestricted inventories, 'he' and 'she', in their quality of pronouns, stand in a special category, relationally defined, with a restricted number of members. The task will then consist in carrying the analysis further until all inventories have been restricted, and restricted as much as possible.

In this reduction of content-entities to "groups," a sign-content is equated with a chain of sign-contents having certain mutual relations. The definitions with which words are translated in a unilingual dictionary are in principle of this kind, although dictionaries have not hitherto aimed at a reduction and therefore do not yield definitions that can be immediately taken over by a consistently performed analysis. But that which is established as equivalent to a given entity, when that entity is so reduced, is actually the *definition* of that entity, formulated in the same language and in the same plane as that to which the entity itself belongs. Nor do we see anything at this point to prevent our applying the same terminology to the two planes and thus also calling it a definition when, for example, the word-expression *pan* is analyzed as consisting of the consonant *p*, the vowel *a*, and the consonant *n*. In this way we are led to the definition of definition: by a *definition* is understood a partition of a sign-content or of a sign-expression.

This reduction of entities to groups of elements can in several cases be made more effectual by the registration of *connectives* as such. By a *connective* we mean a functive that under certain conditions is solidary with complex units of a certain degree. In the expression plane, connectives are in practice often (but by no means always) identical with what in older linguistics were called union vowels, but differ from them by being defined. The vocoid that appears in English before the flexional ending in *fishes* may be registered as a connective. In the content plane the conjunctions, for example, will very often be connectives, a fact that can be of decisive importance for the analysis and inventory of sentences and clauses in languages of a certain structure. For by virtue of this fact we shall ordinarily, already at the stage of analyzing sentences, be able to reach, not merely a resolution of complex sentences into simple clauses, but also a reduction through the whole inventory of a given primary and a given secondary clause to one clause with both functional possibilities. Primary (selected) clause and secondary 66] (selecting) clause will then be, not two kinds of clauses, but two kinds of "clause-functions" or two kinds of clause-variants. We add for the sake of completeness that a specific word order in certain kinds of secondary clauses may be registered as a *signal* for these clause-variants and thus does not prevent the reduction from being carried out.—Moreover, the fate that here overtakes two of the basic pillars of conventional syntax—the primary clause and the secondary clause, which are thus reduced to mere variants—will, in quite corresponding manner, come to befall several others of its basic pillars. In familiar linguistic structures the subject and predicate will be variants of one and the same noun (one and the same junction, or the like). The object, in a language without object case, will be a variant entirely on a line with these, and, in a language with object case, where this has other functions besides, the object will be a variant of a noun in this case. In other words, the distribution of functives into two classes—invariants and variants —that we are undertaking eliminates the conventional bifurcation of linguistics into morphology and syntax.

We must, therefore, register the relation between expression-correlation and content-correlation for all entities of the text in both planes. The distinctive factor is seen to be relevant for all inventorying. A correlation in one plane, which in this way has relation to a correlation in the other plane of a language, we shall call a *commutation*. This is a practical definition; in the theory, we seek, to be sure, a more abstract and more general formulation. Just as we can imagine a correlation and an exchange within a paradigm that have relation to a corresponding correlation and to a corresponding exchange within a paradigm in the other plane of a language, so also we can imagine a relation and a shift within a chain that have relation to a corresponding relation and to a corresponding shift within a chain in the other plane of a language; in such a case we shall speak of a *permutation*. A permutation is frequently found between signs of relatively large extension; and it is even possible to define *words* as minimal permutable signs. As a common term for commutation and permutation we choose *mutation*. Derivates of the same degree belonging to one and the same process or to one and the same system are said to constitute a *rank*, 67] and we define mutation as a function existing between first-degree derivates of one and the same class, a function that has relation to a function between other first-degree derivates of one and the same class and belonging to the same rank. *Commutation* is then a mutation between the members of a paradigm, and *permutation* a mutation between the parts of a chain.

By *substitution* we mean absence of mutation between the members of a paradigm; substitution in our sense is therefore the opposite of commutation. It follows from the definitions that certain entities have neither mutual commutation nor mutual substitution, namely such entities as do not enter into one and the same paradigm; thus, for example, a vowel and a consonant, or *h* and *ŋ* in Jones' example given above.

*Invariants*, then, are correlates with mutual commutation, and *variants* are correlates with mutual substitution.

The specific structure of an individual language, the traits that characterize a given language in contrast to others, that differentiate it from others, that make it similar to others, and that determine the typological place of each language, are established when we specify what relationally defined categories the language has, and what number of invariants enter into each of them. The number of invariants within each category is established by the commutation test. What we have called, with reference to Saussure, linguistic form, which, in different fashion from language to language, lays its arbitrary boundaries on a purport-continuum that is amorphous in itself, depends exclusively on this structure. All the examples we have given (pp. 52 ff.) are precisely so many examples of the relevance of the commutation test; the number of color designations, of numbers, of tenses, of stops, of vowels, *etc.*, *etc.*, is established in this way. The content elements 'tree' and 'wood (material)' are variants in Danish (see page 54) but invariants in German and French; the content-elements 'wood (material)' and 'wood (forest)' are invariants in Danish but variants in French. The content-elements 'large forest' and 'not-large forest' or 'forest without respect to size', are invariants in French but variants in German and

Danish. The only criterion for establishing this is the commutation test.

68] If the older grammar blindly transferred the Latin categories and members of categories into modern European languages, as for example, Danish,[19] this was because the relevance of the commutation test for the linguistic content was not clearly understood. If the linguistic content is treated without any consideration of commutation, the practical result will be its treatment without consideration of its relation through the sign function to the linguistic expression. The result has been that in recent times, as a reaction, we have been led to require a grammatical method that takes its starting point in the expression and seeks to go from there to the content.[20] After the discovery of commutation in its full extent, it turns out that this requirement is inaccurately formulated. With the same right one might require that the study of expression start from the content and proceed from the content to the expression. The important thing is that, whether at the moment we are interested especially in the expression or especially in the content, we understand nothing of the structure of a language if we do not constantly take into first consideration the interplay between the planes. Both the study of expression and the study of content are a study of the relation between expression and content; these two disciplines presuppose each other, are interdependent, and cannot therefore be isolated from each other without serious harm. The analysis must, as we have already said (sections 9–11), be so made that the functions are put at its basis.

## 15. Linguistic schema and linguistic usage

The linguist must be equally interested in the similarity and in the difference between languages, two complementary sides of

[19] On this point see, among others, H. G. Wiwel, *Synspunkter for dansk sproglære*, København, 1901, p. 4.

[20] So, not least, the author of the present work (L. Hjelmslev, *Principes de grammaire générale, Det Kgl. Danske Videnskabernes Selskab, Hist.-filol. Medd.* XVI, 1, København, 1928, especially p. 89).

the same thing. The similarity between languages is their very
structural principle; the difference between languages is the
carrying out of that principle *in concreto*. Both the similarity and
the difference between languages lie, then, in language and in
languages themselves, in their internal structure; and no similarity or difference between languages rests on any factor outside
language. Both the similarity and the difference between languages rest on what, following Saussure, we have called
69]    the form, not on the substance that is formed. The purport that is formed might perhaps *a priori* be supposed to
belong to that which is common to all languages, and thus to the
similarity between languages, but this is an illusion; the purport
is formed in a specific fashion in each language, and therefore no
universal formation is found, but only a universal principle of
formation. In itself purport is unformed, not in itself subjected
to formation but simply susceptible of formation, and of any
formation whatsoever; if boundaries should be found here, they
would lie in the formation, not in the purport. The purport is
therefore in itself inaccessible to knowledge, since the prerequisite for knowledge is an analysis of some kind; the purport can
be known only through some formation, and thus has no scientific existence apart from it.

It is therefore impossible to take the purport—expression-
purport or content-purport—as the basis for linguistic description. If we wished to do that, it would have to be on the basis of
a previous undertaking, a purport-formation set up once and for
all, which, however structured, would inevitably be incongruent
with most languages. This is why both the construction of grammar on speculative ontological systems and the construction of a
given grammar on the grammar of another language are necessarily foredoomed to miscarry.

It is therefore impossible to introduce at the beginning a description of substance as the basis for the description of a language. On the contrary, the description of substance depends
on the description of the linguistic form. The old dream of a uni-

versal phonetic system and a universal content system (system of concepts) cannot therefore be realized, or in any case will remain without any possible contact with linguistic reality. It is not superfluous, in the face of certain offshoots of mediæval philosophy that have appeared even in recent times, to point out the fact that generally valid phonetic types or an eternal scheme of ideas cannot be erected empirically with any validity for language. Differences between languages do not rest on different realizations of a type of substance, but on different realizations of a principle of formation, or, in other words, on a different form in the face of an identical but amorphous purport.

Thus, considerations we have been led to entertain in the foregoing, in direct consequence of Saussure's distinction between form and substance, lead us to recognize that language is a form and that outside that form, with function to it, is present 70] a non-linguistic stuff, Saussure's "substance"—the purport. While it is the business of linguistics to analyze the linguistic form, it will just as inevitably fall to the lot of other sciences to analyze the purport. From a projection of the results of linguistics on the results of these other sciences will come a projection of the linguistic form on the purport in a given language. Since the linguistic formation of the purport is arbitrary, *i.e.*, not based on the purport but on the particular principle of the form and the consequent possibilities of realization, these two descriptions—the linguistic and the non-linguistic—must be undertaken independently of each other.

To make this precise and to give it a plastic, palpable clarity it might be desirable to state which sciences the description of purport belongs to, all the more so because on this point linguistics has up to now been disposed to a vagueness that has deep roots in tradition. Here we may draw attention to two facts:

a) The description of purport, in respect of both the linguistic expression and the linguistic content, may in all essentials be thought of as belonging partly to the sphere of *physics* and partly to that of (social) *anthropology*. (We state this without taking any stand with regard to certain points of contention in modern philosophy.) The substance of both planes can be viewed both as physical entities (sounds in the expression plane, things in the content plane) and as the conception of these entities held by the users of the language. Consequently for both planes both a physical and a phenomenological description of the purport should be required.

b) An exhaustive description of the linguistic content-purport actually requires a collaboration of all the non-linguistic sciences; from our point of view, they all, without exception, deal with a linguistic content.

With the relative justification provided by a particular point of view, we are thus led to regard all science as centered around linguistics. We are led to a simplification that consists in reducing scientific entities to two fundamental sorts, languages and non-languages, and are led to see a relationship, a function between them.

Later we shall have occasion to discuss the nature of this function between language and non-language and to 71] study the kind of entailment and presupposition present in this particular case. At the same time we shall be led to expand and change the image that we have provisionally drawn. What has been said here on this subject, and in particular about Saussure's form and substance, is only provisional.

From the point of view adopted here we must then conclude that, just as the various special, non-linguistic sciences can and must undertake an analysis of the linguistic purport without considering the linguistic form, so linguistics can and must undertake an analysis of the linguistic form without considering the purport that can be ordered to it in both planes. While the content-purport and the expression-purport must be viewed as being sufficiently—and in the only adequate way—described by the non-linguistic sciences, linguistics must be assigned the special task of describing the linguistic form, in order thereby to make possible a projection of it upon the non-linguistic entities which from the point of view of language provide the substance. Linguistics must then see its main task in establishing a science of the expression and a science of the content on an internal and functional basis; it must establish the science of the expression without having recourse to phonetic or phenomenological premisses, the science of the content without ontological or phenomenological premisses (but of course not without the epistemological premisses on which all science rests). Such a linguistics, as distinguished from conventional linguistics, would be one whose science of the expression is not a phonetics and whose science of the content is not a semantics. Such a science would be an algebra of language, operating with unnamed entities, *i.e.*, arbitrarily named entities without natural designation, which would receive a motivated designation only on being confronted with the substance.

Since linguistics is faced with this main task, whose solution has till now been almost completely neglected in all study of language, it must be prepared to face a most comprehensive work of thought and research. So far as linguistic expression is concerned, a beginning of this work in certain limited areas has been made in recent times.[21]

---

[21] A description of categories of the expression on a purely non-phonetic basis has, in particular, been undertaken by L. Bloomfield for English and, partly, for other languages (*Language*, New York, 1933, pp. 130 ff.), by George L. Trager for Polish (*Acta linguistica* I, 1939, p. 179), by Hans Vogt for Norwegian (*Norsk tidsskrift for sprogvidenskap* XII, 1942, pp. 5 ff.), by H. J. Uldall for Danish (*Proceedings of the Second International Congress of Phonetic Sciences*, Cambridge, 1936, pp. 54 ff.) and for Hottentot (*Africa* XII, 1939, pp. 369 ff.), by A. Bjerrum for the Danish dialect in Fjolde (*Fjoldemålets lydsystem*, 1944), by J. Kurylowicz for Ancient Greek (*Travaux du Cercle linguistique de Copenhague* V, 1949, pp. 56 f.), by Knud Togeby for French (*Structure immanente de la langue française*, 1951), and by L. Hjelmslev for Lithuanian (*Studi baltici* VI, 1936–37, pp. 1 ff.) and for Danish (*Selskab for nordisk filologi, Årsberetning for 1948–49–50*, pp. 12–23). Already in Saussure's *Mémoire sur le système primitif des voyelles*, Leipzig, 1879, this point of view is clearly and consciously presented; the method

72]    From its first foundation the present linguistic theory has been inspired by this conception, and it aims to produce just such an immanent algebra of language. To mark its difference from previous kinds of linguistics and its basic independence of non-linguistically defined substance, we have given it a special name, which has been used in preparatory works since 1936: we call it *glossematics* (from γλῶσσα 'a language'), and we use *glossemes* to mean the minimal forms which the theory leads us to establish as bases of explanation, the irreducible invariants. Such a special designation would not have been necessary if *linguistics* had not been so frequently misused as the name for an unsuccessful study of language proceeding from transcendent and irrelevant points of view.

Saussure's distinction between "form" and "substance" has, however, only a relative justification, namely, from the point of view of language. "Form" here means *linguistic form*, and "substance"—as we have seen—linguistic substance, or *purport*. In themselves the concepts "form" and "substance" in a more absolute sense have a more general scope, but they cannot be generalized without risk of terminological obscurity. It must, of course, be expressly emphasized that "substance" does not enter into opposition with the concept of function, but can only designate a whole that is in itself functional and that is related to a given "form" in a certain way, as the purport is related to the linguistic form. But the non-linguistic analysis of the purport, which is undertaken by the non-linguistic sciences, also leads by the very nature of the matter to a recognition of a "form" essentially of the same sort as the linguistic "form," although of non-linguistic nature. We think it possible to suppose that several of the general principles which we are led to set up in the initial stages of linguistic theory are valid not merely for linguistics, but for all science, and not least the principle of the exclusive

is lucidly formulated by his pupil Sechehaye (*Programme et méthodes de la linguistique théorique*, Paris, 1908, pp. 111, 133, 151).

relevance of functions for analysis (p. 23). Then what
73] from one point of view is "substance" is from another
point of view "form," this being connected with the fact
that functives denote only terminals or points of intersection for
functions, and that only the functional net of dependences has
knowability and scientific existence, while "substance," in an
ontological sense, remains a metaphysical concept.

The non-linguistic analysis of purport must, then, through a
deduction (in our sense of the word), lead to the recognition of
a non-linguistic hierarchy, which has function to the linguistic
hierarchy discovered through the linguistic deduction.

We shall call this linguistic hierarchy the *linguistic schema* and
the resultants of the non-linguistic hierarchy, when they are
ordered to a linguistic schema, the *linguistic usage*. We shall
further say that the linguistic usage *manifests* the linguistic
schema, and the function between the linguistic schema and
the linguistic usage we shall call *manifestation*. These terms
stand provisionally as operative.

### 16. Variants in the linguistic schema

In the linguistic schema as well as in the linguistic usage, certain
entities can be reduced to specimens of certain others (*cf.* section
14). Any functive in the linguistic schema can, *within the schema*
and without reference to the manifestation, be subjected to an
articulation into variants. This follows from the very definition
of variant (p. 74). Moreover, the articulation is universal, not
particular (p. 40), since any functive can always be articulated
an unrestricted number of times into an arbitrary number of
variants. Variants are therefore, as a rule, virtual, like the irreducible invariants, according to the given definitions (p. 40),
while reducible invariants alone are realized.

In the modern phonetically oriented science of the expression
it is the custom to distinguish between two kinds of variants—
the so-called "free" variants, which appear independently of the
environments, and the so-called "bound" or "conditioned"

(or—but we shall not recommend this expression—"combinatory") variants, which appear only in certain environments in the chain. If the analysis is carried out thoroughly, any entity of expression can be said to have as many bound variants as it has possible relations in the chain. And, if the analysis is carried out thoroughly, any entity of expression can be said to have as many free variants as it has possible specimens, since, for a sufficiently sensitive experimental-phonetic registration, two specimens of the same speech-sound are never completely the same. The "free" variants we shall here call *variations*, and the "bound" variants *varieties*. *Variations* are defined as combined variants, since they are not presupposed by, and do not presuppose, any definite entities as coexisting in the chain; variations contract combination. *Varieties* are defined as solidary variants, since a given variety always presupposes and is presupposed by a given variety of another invariant (or of another invariant-specimen) in the chain: into the syllable *ta* enter two varieties of two invariants, namely a variety of *t* that can appear only together with *a*, and a variety of *a* that can appear only together with *t*; between them there is a solidarity.

74]

The distribution of the variants into two categories, which is thus suggested by the modern science of the expression, is, as can be seen, of functional importance and must be carried out everywhere. In this connexion, in view of the present situation in linguistics, it is important to emphasize that an articulation into variants is just as possible and necessary in the science of the content as in the science of the expression. All so-called contextual meanings manifest varieties, and special meanings beyond these manifest variations. Moreover, for both planes of a language, in deference to the requirement of the simplest possible description, it is important to insist that the articulation into variations presupposes the articulation into varieties, since an invariant must first be articulated into varieties and after that the varieties into variations: the variations specify the varieties. But it seems possible for a new articulation into varieties to be connected to an exhaustive articulation into variations, and so on; insofar as this is possible, there is a transitive specification.

If the articulation of an invariant into varieties is carried out to each individual "position," an irreducible variety is reached, and the articulation into varieties is exhausted. A variety that thus cannot be further articulated into varieties we shall call a *localized* variety. If the articulation of a localized variety into variations is carried out down to the individual specimen, an irreducible variation is reached, and the articulation into variations is exhausted. A variation that thus cannot be further articulated into variations we shall call an *individual*. Now it will sometimes be possible to articulate an individual again into varieties according to the different "positions" in which the individual can appear; in such cases there is a transitive specification.

75]     The fact that an articulation into variants can be thus exhausted at a given stage does not contradict the virtuality of the variants. On condition of transitive specification the articulation into variants is, in principle, unrestricted. But, besides, the articulation into variants is also unrestricted within its particular stage despite its exhaustibility, because the number of the variants in an unrestricted text will always be unrestricted, and the number of possible articulations through which the articulation into variants, even at the particular stage, can be exhausted will therefore also be unrestricted.

If the transitive specification cannot be continued, and the hierarchy ends as exhausted in an articulation of varieties into variations that cannot again be articulated into varieties, it will be possible to say in a certain epistemological sense that the object under consideration is no longer susceptible of further scientific description. For the aim of science is always to register cohesions, and if an object only presents the possibility of registering constellations or absences of function, exact treatment is no longer possible. To say that the object of science is the registration of cohesions means, if we divest this statement of the terminological wrappings introduced by us, that a science always seeks to comprehend objects as consequences of a reason or as effects of a cause. But if the object can be resolved only into objects that may all indifferently be said to be consequences or effects of all or none, a continued scientific analysis becomes fruitless.

*A priori*, it is not unthinkable that any science attempting to carry out the points of view we have advocated for linguistic theory will, at the conclusion of the deduction, come to face a final situation where no consequences of reasons or effects of causes are perceived. There will then remain as the only possibility a statistics-of-variation treatment, such as Eberhard Zwirner has attempted to carry through systematically for the phonetic expression of languages.[22] If, however, this experiment is to be properly made, what is taken as object of this "phonometric" treatment should not be an inductively discovered class of sounds, but a deductively discovered linguistic localized variety of the highest degree.

We have had occasion above (pp. 72–73) to observe that the entities usually registered by conventional syntax—primary clauses and secondary clauses, members of clauses, like
76]    subject, predicate noun, object, *etc.*—are variants. With the further terminology now introduced, we can add, to be precise, that they are varieties. Conventional syntax (understood as the study of the connexions between words), is, in the main, a study of varieties in the content plane of language, although, as such, it is not exhaustive. Since each articulation of variants presupposes registered invariants, syntax cannot be maintained as an autonomous discipline.

### 17. Function and sum

A class that has function to one or more other classes within the same rank we shall call a *sum*. A syntagmatic sum we shall call a

[22] See the writer, *Nordisk tidsskrift for tale og stemme* II, 1938, especially pp. 179 ff.

*unit*, a paradigmatic sum a *category*. Thus a *unit* is a chain that has relation to one or more other chains within the same rank, and a *category* is a paradigm that has correlation to one or more other paradigms within the same rank. By an *establishment* we understand a relation that exists between a sum and a function entering into it; the function is said to *establish* the sum, and the sum to *be established by* the function. Thus, for example, within the paradigmatic (linguistic system) we can observe the existence of different categories which have mutual correlation and each of which in particular is established by the correlation between its members. This correlation, in the case of the categories of invariants, is a commutation; in the case of the categories of variants it is a substitution. Likewise in the syntagmatic (the linguistic process, the text) we can observe the existence of different units which have mutual relation and each of which in particular is established by the relation between its parts.

It follows from the definitions that functions always are present either between sums or between functions; in other words, every entity is a sum. A contributory factor in making possible this point of view is, of course, that the number of the variants is unrestricted and that the articulation into variants can be continued indefinitely, so that each entity may be considered as a sum, namely, in every case, as a sum of variants. The point of view is made necessary by the requirement of an exhaustive description.

In the theory this means that an entity is nothing else than two or more entities with mutual function, a result that further underlines the fact that only the functions have scientific existence (p. 23).

77]   In practice it is especially important in the analysis to understand that relation is present between categories only.

The analysis must so proceed that first the appropriate basis of analysis is chosen with reference to the empirical principle and the principles derived therefrom. Let us imagine that selection is chosen as the basis of analysis. Then in the first operation the given chain is analyzed into first-degree selection-units; the category that is obtained from all these units we call the *functional category*. By this, then, is understood the category of the functives that are registered in a single analysis with a given function taken as the basis of analysis. Within such a functional category four kinds of functives may be imagined:

1. functives that can appear only as selected;
2. functives that can appear only as selecting;
3. functives that can appear both as selected and as selecting;
4. functives that can appear neither as selected nor as selecting (*i.e.*, functives that contract only solidarities and/or combinations, or that do not contract relation at all).

Each of these four categories we shall call a *functival category;* thus, by functival categories we mean the categories that are registered by articulation of a functional category according to functival possibilities. The operation of the analysis consists in investigating which of these four *a priori* possible functival categories are realized and which are virtual—by analyzing each of the functival categories into members on the basis of the commutation test; these members we have called *elements*. If the analysis is a partition into first-degree selectional units, the elements are the particular first-degree selectional units that the partition leads to registering.

Let us again imagine as a concrete example a partition of the chain into primary clauses and secondary clauses. The primary clauses will belong to functival category 1, the secondary clauses to functival category 2. For the sake of simplification let us imagine that functival categories 3 and 4 both prove to be virtual. Now it is clear that this registration cannot mean that each particular secondary clause selects each particular primary clause: a particular secondary clause does not require the presence of a certain primary clause, but only of some primary clause or

another. Thus it is the category of primary clauses that
78]    is selected by the category of secondary clauses; the selection exists between the functival categories, while the
relation that exists as a consequence thereof between a member
of one functival category and a member of the other may well
be different—a combination, for example. It is part of the task
of linguistics to set up a general calculus for the relations between elements that correspond to given relations between functival categories.

If the basis of analysis is solidarity or combination, *i.e.*, a syntagmatic reciprocity, the functival categories will be:

1. functives that can appear only as solidary;
2. functives that can appear only as combined;
3. functives that can appear both as solidary and as combined;
4. functives that can appear neither as solidary nor as combined
   (*i.e.*, functives that contract only selections or that do not
   contract any relation at all).

Here, in like manner, solidarity or combination will be present
between the functival categories, while the elements can have
other relations. We have seen an example of this above (p. 27)
in the discussion of the Latin nominal morphemes: the category
of number and the category of case have mutual solidarity, but
there is combination between any particular number and any
particular case.

## 18. Syncretism

We shall now be able to consider that phenomenon which is
known in conventional grammar as *syncretism* and in modern
phonemics as *neutralization*, and which consists in the fact that
the commutation between two invariants may be suspended
under given conditions. Familiar examples, which we may well
retain here, are the syncretism in Latin between nominative and
accusative in the neuter (and in certain other instances), and the

neutralization that is found in Danish between $p$ and $b$ in the final part of the syllable (so that a word like *top* may be pronounced with a $p$ or $b$ indifferently).

For such instances we shall use the term *suspension*, and we introduce the following general definition: given a functive that is present under certain conditions and absent under certain other conditions, then, under the conditions where the functive is present, there is said to be *application* of the functive, 79]   and under these conditions the functive is said to *apply*, while under the conditions where the functive is absent there is said to be *suspension* or *absence* of the functive, so that the functive is said to be *suspended* or *absent* under these conditions.

A suspended mutation between two functives we call an *overlapping*, and the category that is established by an overlapping we call (in both planes of a language) a *syncretism*. Thus, for example, we say that nominative and accusative in Latin, or $p$ and $b$ in Danish, have mutual overlapping, or contract overlapping, and that these entities together with their overlapping constitute a syncretism, or that each of the entities enters into a syncretism.

It follows from the definitions that when two entities under certain conditions are registered as invariants on the basis of the commutation test, and under other conditions contract overlapping, then under these other conditions they will be variants while only their syncretism will be an invariant. In both instances the conditions lie in the relations which the given entities contract in the chain: the commutation between nominative and accusative in Latin (which applies, *e.g.*, in the first declension) is suspended when, for example, nominative and/or accusative contract(s) relation with neuter; and the commutation between $p$ and $b$ in Danish (which applies, *e.g.*, in initial position: *pære* 'pear'—*bære* 'carry') is suspended when, for example, $p$ and/or $b$ contract(s) relation with a preceding central part of a syllable.

It is necessary to understand that the relation that is relevant in these instances is a relation to *variants*. The entity whose presence is a necessary condition for the overlapping between nominative and accusative is the variety of neuter that is solidary with nominative-accusative; and the entity whose presence is a necessary condition for the overlapping between *p* and *b* is the variety of central part of a syllable that is solidary with a following *p/b*.

Such a solidarity between a variant on the one hand and an overlapping on the other hand we call a *dominance;* we say that the given variant *dominates* the overlapping, and that the overlapping *is dominated by* the given variant.[23]

80]      The special advantage of setting up the formal definitions in this way is that we may further distinguish between obligatory and optional dominance without having to have recourse to the sociological presuppositions that the "real" definition of these terms would necessarily involve, and which would at best mean a complication of the apparatus of premises in the theory and thus conflict with the principle of simplicity, and at worst would perhaps even involve metaphysical premises and thus in a further sense conflict with the empirical principle and especially with the requirement of giving completely explicit definitions. Concepts like obligatory and optional would, according to their hitherto adopted, explicit or implicit, "real" definitions, necessarily presuppose a concept of sociological norm, which proves to be dispensable throughout linguistic theory. We can now simply define an *obligatory* dominance as a dominance in which the dominant in respect to the syncretism is a *variety*, and an *optional* dominance as a dominance in which the dominant in respect of the syncretism is a *variation;* when, under certain circumstances, the overlapping is obligatory, there is a solidarity between the dominant on the one hand and on the other hand the syncretism, the category of the entities

---

[23] Instead of *dominance*, in the examples chosen here, we can use a more specific term and speak of *syncretization*, since *dominance* can be generalized to be valid also for defectiveness.

that can contract the overlapping; when, under certain conditions, the overlapping is optional, there is a combination between the dominant and the syncretism.

Syncretisms can be manifested in two different ways: as *fusions* or *implications*. By a fusion we mean a manifestation of a syncretism which, from the point of view of the substance-hierarchy, is identical with the manifestation either of all or of none of the functives that enter into the syncretism. The syncretisms used as examples above are manifested as fusions in which the manifestation of the syncretism is identical with the manifestation of all (both) the functives that enter into the syncretism. Thus the syncretism of nominative and accusative has the meaning 'nominative-accusative' (in different contexts this meaning involves the variety-manifestations that nominative and accusative have usually); so also the syncretism $p/b$ is pronounced in the same way as $p$ and $b$ are usually pronounced (in different connexions with the same variety-manifestations). An example of a syncretism where the manifestation is not identical with the manifestation of any of the functives that enter 81]  into the syncretism is found in the overlapping of different vowels under certain accentual conditions in Russian and in English, where the syncretism is pronounced [ə]. By an *implication* we mean a manifestation of a syncretism which, from the point of view of the substance-hierarchy, is identical with the manifestation of one or more of the functives that enter into the syncretism but not with all. If in a language voiced and voiceless consonant are commutable, but their commutation is suspended before another consonant so that a voiceless consonant is pronounced voiced before a voiced consonant, there is an implication. Of the functives that contract implication that (or those) whose manifestation is identical with that of the syncretism is (are) said to *be implied by* that (or those) other functive(s), and the latter is (are) said to *imply* that (or those) functive(s) whose manifestation is identical with that of the syncretism. Thus in the example chosen we shall say that a voiceless consonant under certain conditions implies a voiced consonant, or that a voiced consonant under these conditions is implied by a voiceless. If the syncretism between voiced and voiceless consonant takes place in such a way (as is common, for example, in the Slavonic languages) that not only a voiceless consonant has a voiced pronunciation before a voiced consonant, but also a voiced consonant has a voiceless pronunciation before a voiceless consonant, the implication is not *unilateral* but *multilateral* (*bilateral*), voiced implies voiceless, and voiceless implies voiced, under mutually exclusive conditions.

We draw attention to the fact that this use of the term *implication* agrees with that of logistics and is only a special instance of it. Implication is an if-then function, an entailment, with the only difference that in our examples it is not between propositions but between entities of smaller extension; *if* we have the glossematic expression-entity *p* in a certain relation to another such entity, *then* we get *q*. Logical entailment between propositions seems to us merely another special case of linguistic implication.[24]

A syncretism can be *resoluble* or *irresoluble*. To *resolve* a syncretism means to introduce the syncretism-variety which does not contract the overlapping that establishes the syncretism. If, despite the syncretism, we can explain *templum* in one context as nominative and in another context as accusative, that is because the Latin syncretism of nominative and accusative in these instances is *resoluble;* we perform the resolution within the category of nominative and accusative, thus within the syncretism, by selecting a variety that does not contract overlapping (*e.g.*, the nominative variety from *domus* and the accusative variety from *domum*) and by artificially introducing this content-entity into *templum* instead of the case-entity that enters therein; this is done on the strength of an analogical inference that rests on the application of the generalization principle. A syncretism is resoluble only if such analogical

82]

---

[24] The resemblance is made all the closer when propositions are considered as composite names; see J. Jørgensen, *The Journal of Unified Science* VIII, 1939, pp. 233 f. and IX, 1940, pp. 185 ff.

inferences are possible on the basis of the results which the analysis of the linguistic schema provides. Such generalizing analogical inferences are not possible in the case of *top*, and consequently we must here declare the syncretism $p/b$ irresoluble.

A chain with unresolved resoluble syncretisms may be called *actualized*, and a chain with resolved resoluble syncretisms *ideal*. This distinction is relevant to the distinction between a narrow and a broad notation of the expression, and both these kinds of notation are thus possible on the basis of the analysis of the linguistic schema.

When we resolve a syncretism and make an ideal notation, the noting (writing down or pronunciation) of the syncretism, represented as it is by one of its members, will in itself be an implication, in which the syncretism implies the given member. It seems to us that this will be relevant to an analysis of logical conclusion, which is, after all, in the conception of modern logicians, a purely linguistic operation and therefore also might be able to expect elucidation from linguistic premisses. In the foregoing (p. 32) we have thought it possible to define a logical conclusion as an analysis of a premised proposition. We can now add the more precise statement that the premised proposition may obviously be viewed as a resoluble syncretism of its consequences; a logical conclusion, then, is an articulation of the premised proposition, an articulation consisting in a resolution of the given syncretism which appears as an implication.

In general it seems to us that the concept of syncretism which has been reached from internal linguistic premisses might with advantage be used to cast light on various supposedly non-linguistic phenomena. In this way, perhaps, it will be possible to cast a certain light on the general problem of the relationship between class and segment. Insofar as a paradigm is considered not as a mere addition of its members (*class as many* in Russell's terminology), but as something different from its members (*class as one*) it is a syncretism of its members; by the resolution of the syncretism a *class as one* is transformed into a *class as many*. It should consequently be clear that insofar as we may try to attach a scientific meaning to the word *concept*, we must understand by a concept a syncretism between things (namely, the things that the concept subsumes).

Into a syncretism may enter, besides explicit entities, the zero entity, which has a quite special significance for linguistic analysis. The necessity has often been noted of recognizing the existence of *latent* and *facultative* linguistic entities, especially "phonemes."[25] Thus, on the basis of certain analytical results, one can maintain the existence of a latent $d/t$ in French *grand, sourd* because a $d$ or a $t$ appears in these expressions when the conditions are changed: *grande, sourde; grand homme*. Likewise one will be able to maintain the facultativity of $\gamma$ in Danish after $i$ and $u$ (*yndig, kugle*). A moment's reflexion is enough to show that latency and facultativity cannot be defined as suspended manifestation; the functions in question are grounded in the linguistic schema, since the conditions under which latency and facultativity appear are fixed by relations in the chain and rest on dominance. Latency and facultativity must then be understood as overlapping with zero. *Latency* is an overlapping with zero in which the dominance is obligatory (since the dominant in respect to the syncretism is a variety), and a functive that contracts latency is called *latent*. *Facultativity* is an overlapping with zero in which the dominance is optional (since the dominant in respect of the syncretism is a variation), and a functive that contracts facultativity is called *facultative*.

### 19. Catalysis

As we have seen (sections 9–11), the analysis consists in a registration of functions. When this point of view is adopted, the possibility must be foreseen that the registration of certain

84] functions may, by virtue of the solidarity between func-

[25] J. Baudouin de Courtenay, "Fakultative Sprachlaute" (*Donum natalicium Schrijnen*, 1929, pp. 38 ff.). A. Martinet has operated with a latent $h$ in analyzing French (*Bulletin de la Société de linguistique de Paris* XXXIV, 1933, pp. 201 f.).

tion and functive, oblige us to interpolate certain functives which would in no other way be accessible to knowledge. This interpolation we call *catalysis*.

In practice, catalysis is a necessary condition for carrying out the analysis. The analysis of Latin, for example, must lead us to the result that the preposition *sine* selects (governs) the ablative (p. 26), that is to say, according to the definitions, that the presence of an ablative in the text is a necessary condition for the presence of *sine* (but not *vice versa*). It is clear that such a result cannot be reached by a mere mechanical observation of the entities that enter into the actual texts. We can very easily imagine an actual text in which *sine* appears without an accompanying ablative, a text, for example, which for one reason or another is interrupted or incomplete (a damaged inscription, a fragment, an unfinished written or oral utterance). In general, the registration of any cohesion must presuppose that such incalculable accidents in the exercise of language (*accidents de la parole*) are first eliminated. And the phenomena in actual texts that would prevent a mechanical registration of connexions are not limited to this sort of unintentional disturbances. It is well known that both aposiopesis and abbreviation enter as a constant and essential part into the economy of linguistic usage (one may think of utterances like: *How nice! If I only had! Because!*, *etc., etc.*). If in the analysis one were reduced to registering relations on this basis one would end up in all likelihood (contrary to the purpose of science, *cf.* p. 83) merely registering pure combinations.

The requirement of an exhaustive description, however, obliges us, while we register these aposiopeses and the like, also to recognize them as such, since the analysis must likewise register the outward relations which the actually observed entities have, the cohesions that point beyond the given entity and to something outside it. If we are faced with a Latin text that breaks off with a *sine*, we can still register a cohesion (selection) with an ablative, *i.e.*, the prerequisite for *sine* may be interpolated, and correspondingly in all other instances. This interpolation of a reason behind a consequence is made in accordance with the generalization principle.

85]     On the other hand, in catalysis we must take care not to supply more in the text than what there is clear evidence for. In the case of *sine* we know with certainty that an ablative is required; and we further know that a Latin ablative too has its prerequisites: it requires the coexistence of certain other morphemes in the chain; and we know concerning the morpheme chain that appears with the ablative that it presupposes the coexistence of a theme. Since, however, the ablative is not solidary with any particular morpheme in each category, but only with certain categories of morphemes (p. 86), and since a morpheme-chain including a case, a number, and a gender, together, in some instances, with a morpheme of comparison, has no cohesions with any particular nominal theme but with the category of all nominal themes, we are not justified in introducing by catalysis any particular noun in the ablative with the given *sine*. What is introduced by catalysis is, then, in most instances not some particular entity but an irresoluble syncretism between all the entities that might be considered possible in the given "place" in the chain. In the case of *sine* we are so fortunate as to know that it is an ablative and only an ablative that can be considered a prerequisite; but as to the entities that the ablative itself requires, we know only that they are some number or other, some gender or other, some morpheme of comparison or other (of course, within the possibilities of the Latin inventory), and some theme or other. In actual fact it presupposes any one of these entities indifferently, and the catalysis must therefore go no farther than to observe the fact.

*Catalysis* we define as a registration of cohesions through the replacement of one entity by another to which it has substitution. In our example *sine* is the replaced entity, *sine* + ablative (+ the cohesive syncretisms) the replacing entity. The replacing entity is thus always equal to the replaced (*catalyzed*) entity + an

interpolated or supplied (*encatalyzed*) entity. As we have seen,
it is true of the encatalyzed entity that it is often, but not necessarily, a syncretism, and, further, that it is often, but not necessarily, latent (latent entities can be registered only by a catalysis,
on application of the principle of generalization), and finally,
that it always and necessarily, if it is an entity of content, has
the expression zero and, if it is an entity of expression, has the
content zero: this last is a consequence of the requirement, con-
tained in the definition, of substitution between the replaced and
the replacing entity.

86]   *20. Entities of the analysis*

Essentially on the basis of the considerations and definitions
that have been stated in the preceding sections of the present
essay, made precise and supplemented by the necessary number
of rules of a more technical sort, linguistic theory prescribes a
*textual analysis*, which leads us to recognize a linguistic form behind the "substance" immediately accessible to observation by
the senses, and behind the text a language (system) consisting
of *categories* from whose definitions can be deduced the possible
*units* of the language. The kernel of this procedure is a catalysis
through which the form is encatalyzed to the substance, and the
language encatalyzed to the text. The procedure is purely formal
in this sense that it considers the units of a language as consisting
of a number of figuræ for which certain rules of transformation
hold. These rules are set up without consideration of the substance in which the figuræ and units are manifested; the linguistic hierarchy and, consequently, the linguistic deduction as
well are independent of the physical and physiological and, in
general, of the non-linguistic hierarchies and deductions that
might lead to a description of the "substance." Therefore one
must not expect from this deductive procedure any semantics or
any phonetics, but both for the expression of a language and for
the content of a language only a "linguistic algebra," which provides the formal basis for an ordering of deductions of non-

linguistic "substance." The "algebraic" entities with which the procedure operates have no natural designation, but must of course be named in one way or another; this naming is arbitrary and appropriate, in harmony with the whole character of linguistic theory. In the arbitrariness of the names lies the fact that they do not at all involve the manifestation; in their appropriateness lies the fact that they are chosen so that it becomes possible to order the information concerning the manifestation in the simplest possible way. On the basis of the arbitrary relation between form and substance, one and the same entity of linguistic form may be manifested by quite different substance-forms, as one passes from one language to another; the projection of the form-hierarchy on the substance-hierarchy can differ essentially from language to language.

The procedure is governed by the basic principles (pp. 11, 18, 61, 69–70), from which we can further deduce, especially for use in textual analysis, the following principle, which we call the *principle of exhaustive description*:

87] *Any analysis (or analysis-complex) in which functives are registered with a given function as basis of analysis shall be so made that it leads self-consistently to the registration of the highest possible number of realized functival categories within the highest possible number of functional categories.*

In practice it follows from this principle that in analyzing a text we must not omit any stage of analysis that might be expected to give functional return (*cf.* p. 59) and that the analysis must move from the invariants that have the greatest extension conceivable to the invariants that have the least extension conceivable, so that between these two extreme points as many derivative degrees are traversed as possible.

Already on this point the analysis differs essentially from the traditional one. For the latter is concerned neither with those parts of the text that have very great extension nor with those that have very small extension. An explicit or implicit tradition has it that the work of the linguist begins with dividing sentences into clauses, while it is thought possible to refer the treat-ment of larger parts of the text, groups of sentences and the like, to other sciences—principally logic and psychology. According to this view the linguist or the grammarian should, when faced with an unanalyzed text, as, for example, the one that is provided by all that is written and said in Danish, be able to plunge head-long down to a stage where it is resolved into clauses; theoreti-cally he must supposedly premise that a logico-psychological analysis of the larger parts of the text has been undertaken, but it is nevertheless believed that in practice he does not have to worry about whether or not such an analysis actually has been undertaken, or whether it has been made in a way that may be called satisfactory from the linguist's point of view.

The question we are raising here is not a question of practical division of labor but of the placing of objects by their definitions. From this point of view the analysis of the text falls to the linguist as an inevitable duty, including the textual parts that have large extension. A partition of the text is attempted with selection and reciprocity as bases of division, and at each stage of the analysis those parts shall be sought that have the greatest extension. And it is easy to see that a linguistic text of very large or unrestricted extension offers the possibility of partition into parts of large extension defined by mutual selection, 88]  solidarity, or combination. The very first of these parti-tions is the partition into content line and expression line, which are solidary. When these are each further partitioned, it will be possible and necessary, *inter alia*, to analyze the content line into literary genres and then to analyze the sciences into premising (selecting) and premised (selected). The systematics of the study of literature and of general science thus find their natural place within the framework of linguistic theory, and under the analysis of the sciences linguistic theory must come to contain within itself its own definition. At a more advanced stage of the procedure the larger textual parts must be further partitioned into productions of single authors, works, chapters, paragraphs, and the like, on the basis of premission, and then in the same way into sentences and clauses. At this point, *inter alia*, syllogisms will be analyzed into premisses and conclusions —obviously a stage of the linguistic analysis in which formal logic must place an important part of its problems. In all this is seen a significant broadening of the perspective, frames and capacities of linguistic theory, and a basis for a motivated and organized collaboration between linguistics in the narrower sense and a number of other disciplines which till now, obviously more or less wrongly, have usually been considered as lying outside the sphere of linguistic science.

In the final operations of the analysis linguistic theory will lead to a partition descending to entities of smaller extension than those which until now have been viewed as the irreducible invariants. This is true not merely in the content plane, where we have seen that conventional linguistics is very far from having carried the analysis to the end, but also in the expression plane. In both planes the partition based on relation will reach a stage in which selection is used for the last time as the basis of analysis. The analysis at this stage will lead to an inventorying of *taxemes*, which will be virtual elements; for the expression plane the taxemes will *grosso modo* be the linguistic forms that are manifested by phonemes, but in this connexion the reservation must be made that an analysis carried out strictly according to the simplicity principle often leads to essentially different results from the phonemic analyses hitherto attempted. It is known that these taxemes as a rule may be further partitioned on the basis of a *universal* division, which appears when they are ordered on the basis of special rules into systems of

89]     two, three, or more dimensions.[26] We cannot here enter into these special rules, which rest on the fact that the linguistic elements in one and the same category are not only

---

[26] See, for example, the systems established in the author's *La Catégorie des cas* I-II (*Acta Jutlandica* VII, 1 and IX, 2, 1935-37). Corresponding systems may be established for the expression plane.

numerically but also qualitatively different.[27] We must be content with indicating merely in principle the fact till now unobserved by linguists, that when a taxeme inventory is "set up into a system" the logical consequence is a further partition of the individual taxeme. Let us, for example, imagine that a category is registered with an inventory of 9 taxemes, and that, from the special rules for qualitative division, these may be set up into a two-dimensional system with three members in each dimension so that the 9 may be described as a product of $3 \times 3$. The members of the dimensions will then themselves be parts of taxemes since each of the 9 taxemes now appears as a unit including one member of the one dimension and one member of the other dimension. The 9 taxemes may accordingly be described as products of $3 + 3 = 6$ invariants, namely the members of the dimensions, and we thus reach a simpler description and satisfy to a higher degree the refined principle of reduction (p. 61). The two dimensions will, as categories, be solidary, and each member in the one dimension will have combination with each member in the other dimension. The members of the dimensions will thus appear as taxeme-parts and as the irreducible invariants. Whether such a "setting up into a system" of a taxeme inventory may be carried out depends essentially on the size of the inventory. When it may be carried out, it will be the members of the dimensions and not the taxemes that are the end-points of the analysis; these end-points we call *glossemes*, and if we assume that one taxeme of expression is usually manifested by one phoneme, then a glosseme of expression will usually be manifested by a part of a phoneme.

After the syntagmatic deduction of the textual analysis is brought to an end, a paradigmatic deduction is undertaken.

[27] See *La catégorie des cas* I, pp. 112 ff. *Cf.* Jens Holt, *Etudes d'aspect* (*Acta Jutlandica* XV, 2, 1943), pp. 26 f. A comprehensive presentation of this side of linguistic theory (given in the Linguistic Circle, on April 27, 1933) will be published under the title *Structure générale des systèmes grammaticaux* in the *Travaux du Cercle linguistique de Copenhague*.

Here the language is articulated into *categories*, into which the
highest-degree taxeme categories of the textual analysis
90]     are distributed, and from which, through a synthesis, can
be deduced the possible *units* of the language. It turns
out that the two sides (the planes) of a language have completely
analogous categorical structure, a discovery that seems to us of
far-reaching significance for an understanding of the structural
principle of a language or in general of the "essence" of a semiotic. It also appears that such a consistently carried out description of a language on the basis of the empirical principle does not
contain the possibility of a syntax or of a science of parts of
speech; as we have seen, the entities of syntax are for the greatest part varieties, and the "parts of speech" of ancient grammar
are entities which will be rediscovered in redefined form in far
different places within the hierarchy of the units.

The science of categories, however, presupposes such a comprehensive and such a closely coherent apparatus of terms and
definitions that its details cannot be described without its being
presented completely; it cannot therefore, any more than the
science of units which determines it, be treated in the prolegomena of the theory.

### 21. *Language and non-language*

In respect of the choice and delimitation of objects we have in
the preceding sections (*cf.* p . 20) followed the prevalent concept
of linguistics and considered *"natural" language* as the unique
object of linguistic theory. But at the same time (p. 20) we have
held out a prospect of widening our point of view, and it is now
time to undertake this in the following sections (21–23). In doing
this we stress that these further perspectives do not come as
arbitrary and dispensable appendages, but that, on the contrary, and *precisely when we restrict ourselves to the pure consideration of "natural" language*, they spring with necessity from
"natural" language and obtrude themselves with inevitable
logical consequence. If the linguist wishes to make clear to him-

self the object of his own science he sees himself forced into
spheres which according to the traditional view are not his. This
fact has, in a way, already left its mark on our presentation thus
far, which, starting from special premisses, has been forced by
the technical posing of the problem into a more general epistemological setting.

Actually it is at once clear that not only the quite general considerations we have been led to make, but also the appar-
91]    ently more special terms we have introduced are applicable to both "natural" language and language in a far
broader sense. Precisely because the theory is so constructed
that linguistic form is viewed without regard for "the substance"
(purport), it will be possible to apply our apparatus to any
structure whose form is analogous to that of a "natural"
language. Our examples have been taken from such language,
and we ourself have proceeded from it, but what we are led to
set up and what we have exemplified is evidently not specific to
"natural" language but has a wider range. A similar universal
applicability to sign systems (or to figuræ systems with sign-
purpose) as a whole is found in the study of functions and their
analysis (sections 9–11, 17), of signs (section 12), of expression
and content, form, substance and purport (sections 13, 15), of
commutation and substitution, variants and invariants and
the classification of variants (sections 14, 16), of class and segment (sections 10, 18), and of catalysis (section 19). In other
words "natural" language may be described on the basis of a
theory which is minimally specific and which must imply further
consequences.

We have already been obliged to show this on occasion. We
have thought it possible to maintain the universal character of
the concepts "process" and "system" and of their interplay
(p. 9), and our view of "natural" language has led us to include
in the theory of language important aspects of literary science,
general philosophy of science, and formal logic (pp. 98–99), and
we have been unable to avoid making some almost inevitable

remarks about the nature of logical conclusion (pp. 32, 91, 92).

At the same time we have been led to view a great number of special sciences outside linguistics as providing the science of linguistic content-purport and we have been led to draw a line between language and non-language (p. 78), whose provisional character we have, however, stressed.

The linguistic theory we have set up stands or falls with the principle on which it is based, which we have called the empirical principle (p. 11). This leads us to accept as a logical necessity (with the necessary reservations concerning the terminology itself, *cf.* pp. 50, 78) Saussure's distinction between form and "substance" (purport), from which it further follows that *"substance" cannot in itself be a definiens for a language.* We must be able to imagine as ordered to one and the same linguistic form substances which, from the point of view of the substance-hierarchy, are essentially different; the arbitrary relation between linguistic form and purport makes this a logical necessity.

92] The long supremacy of conventional phonetics has, moreover, had the effect of restricting the linguists' conception even of "natural" language in a way that is demonstrably unempirical, *i.e.*, inappropriate because non-exhaustive. It has been supposed that the expression-substance of a spoken language must consist exclusively of "sounds." Thus, as has been pointed out by the Zwirners in particular, the fact has been overlooked that speech is accompanied by, and that certain components of speech can be replaced by, gesture, and that in reality, as the Zwirners say, not only the so-called organs of speech (throat, mouth, and nose), but very nearly all the striate musculature, cooperate in the exercise of "natural" language.[28]

Further, it is possible to replace the usual sound-and-gesture substance with any other that offers itself as appropriate under changed external circumstances. Thus the same linguistic form may also be manifested in writing, as happens with a phonetic

[28] Eberhard Zwirner & Kurt Zwirner, *Archives néerlandaises de phonétique expérimentale* XIII, 1937, p. 112.

or phonemic notation and with the so-called phonetic orthographies, as for example the Finnish. Here is a graphic "substance" which is addressed exclusively to the eye and which need not be transposed into a phonetic "substance" in order to be grasped or understood. And this graphic "substance" can, precisely from the point of view of the substance, be of quite various sorts. There can be other "substances," too; we need only think of the navy flag codes, which can very well be used to manifest a "natural" language, *e.g.*, English, or of the sign language of deaf-mutes.

Two opinions are often maintained in opposition to the one here presented. One is that all these substances are "derived" in relation to the sound-and-gesture substance and "artificial" in contrast to the "naturalness" of the latter; there can even, it is said, be many degrees of such "derivations," as when a flag code or a sign language is derived from writing, which is in turn derived from the "natural" spoken language. The other opinion is that a different "substance" is accompanied in many instances by a changed linguistic form; thus not all orthographies are "phonetic" but would, on analysis, lead us to set up a different taxeme inventory and perhaps partly different categories from those of the spoken language.

93]     The first of these opinions is irrelevant, because the fact that a manifestation is "derived" in respect of another does not alter the fact that it *is* a manifestation of the given linguistic form. Moreover it is not always certain what is derived and what not; we must not forget that the discovery of alphabetic writing is hidden in pre-history,[29] so that the assertion that it rests on a phonetic analysis is only one of the possible diachronic hypotheses; it may also have rested on a formal analysis of linguistic structure.[30] But in any case, as is recognized by

[29] Bertrand Russell quite rightly calls attention to the fact that we have no means of deciding whether writing or speech is the older form of human expression (*An Outline of Philosophy*, London, 1927, p. 47).

[30] On this point see the author, *Archiv für vergleichende Phonetik* II, 1938, pp. 211 f.

modern linguistics, diachronic considerations are irrelevant for synchronic description.

The other opinion is irrelevant because it does not alter the general fact that a linguistic form is manifested in the given substance. The observation is interesting, however, in showing that different systems of expression can correspond to one and the same system of content. Accordingly, the task of the linguistic theoretician is not merely that of describing the actually present expression system, but of calculating what expression systems in general are possible as expression for a given content system, *and vice versa*. But it is an experimentally demonstrable fact that any linguistic expression system may be manifested in widely different expression-substances.[31]

Thus, various phonetic usages and various written usages can be ordered to the expression system of one and the same linguistic schema. A language can suffer a change of a purely phonetic nature without having the expression system of the linguistic schema affected, and similarly it can suffer a change of a purely semantic nature without having the content system 94] affected. Only in this way is it possible to distinguish between *phonetic shifts* and *semantic shifts* on the one hand, and *formal shifts* on the other.

From our whole basic point of view there is really nothing surprising in all this. The entities of linguistic form are of "algebraic" nature and have no natural designation; they can therefore be designated arbitrarily in many different ways.

These different possible designations by the substance do not

---

[31] On the relation between writing and speech see A. Penttilä & U. Saarnio in *Erkenntnis* IV, 1934, pp. 28 ff., and H. J. Uldall in *Congrès international des sciences anthropologiques et ethnologiques, Compte rendu de la deuxième session*, København, 1939, p. 374. For older treatments and analyses of writing from a structural point of view, see especially J. Baudouin de Courtenay, *Ob otnošenii russkogo pis'ma k russkomu jazyku*, St. Petersburg, 1912, and *Vvedenie v jazykovedenie*, 4th ed., 1912, pp. 15 ff., and F. de Saussure, *Cours*, 2nd ed., especially p. 165. *Cf.* also an article, with a somewhat unclear treatment of the problem, by Josef Vachek, *Zum Problem der geschriebenen Sprache* (*Travaux du Cercle linguistique de Prague* VIII, 1939, pp. 94 ff.). An analysis of writing without regard to sound has not yet been undertaken.

affect the theory of the linguistic schema. Its attitude does not depend on them. The theoretician's main task is to determine by definition the structural principle of language, from which can be deduced a general calculus in the form of a typology whose categories are the individual languages, or rather, the individual language types. All possibilities must here be foreseen, including those that are virtual in the world of experience, or remain without a "natural" or "actual" manifestation.

In this general calculus there is no question of whether the individual structural types are manifested, but only whether they are manifestable and, *nota bene*, manifestable in any substance whatsoever. Substance is thus not a necessary presupposition for linguistic form, but linguistic form is a necessary presupposition for substance. *Manifestation*, in other words, is a selection in which the linguistic form is the constant and the substance the variable; we formally define manifestation as a selection between hierarchies and between derivates of different hierarchies. The constant in a manifestation (the *manifested*) can, with reference to Saussure, be called the *form;* if the form is a language, we call it the *linguistic schema.*[32] The variable in a manifestation (the *manifesting*) can, in agreement with Saussure, be called the *substance;* a substance that manifests a linguistic schema we call a *linguistic usage.*

From these premises we are led to the formal definition of a *semiotic* as a *hierarchy, any of whose components admits of a further analysis into classes defined by mutual relation, so that any of these classes admits of an analysis into derivates defined by mutual mutation.*

This definition, which is nothing else than the formal consequence of everything we have developed up to this point, obliges the linguist to consider as his subject, not merely "natural,"

---

[32] *Schema* has been adopted here in preference to *pattern*, suggested in my article "Langue et parole" (*Cahiers Ferdinand de Saussure* II, 1942, p. 43; *Essais linguistiques*, p. 81).

everyday language, but any semiotic—any structure that
95]   is analogous to a language and satisfies the given definition. A language (in the ordinary sense) may be viewed
as a special case of this more general object, and its specific characteristics, which concern only linguistic usage, do not affect the
given definition.

Here again we wish to add that it is not so much a question
of the practical division of labor as of the fixing of the object by
definition. The linguist can and should concentrate on "natural"
languages in his research work and leave to others, who have
better preparation than he, mainly to logicians, the investigation
of other semiotic structures. But the linguist cannot with im-
punity study language without the wider horizon that ensures
his proper orientation towards these analogous structures. He
can even derive a practical advantage therefrom, because some
of these structures are simpler in their construction than languages, and they are therefore suitable as models in preparatory
study. Besides, on purely linguistic premisses, it has become
clear that a particularly intimate collaboration is required here
between logistics and linguistics.

Since the time of Saussure it has been known from the linguistic side that language cannot be studied in isolation. Saussure
required, as basis for linguistics in the narrower sense, a discipline
that he christened *semiology* (from σημεῖον 'a sign'). Therefore,
in the years before the second world war, in individual linguistic
or linguistically oriented circles that were interested in the study
of foundations (particularly in Czechoslovakia), significant attempts were made to study other sign systems than languages—
in particular, folk-costume, art, and literature—on a more general semiological basis.[33]

[33] *Cf.*, *inter alia*, P. Bogatyrev, *Příspěvek k strukturální etnografii* (*Slovenská
miscellanea*, Bratislava, 1931); *id.*, *Funkčno-štrukturálna metoda a iné metody
etnografie i folkloristiky* (*Slovenské pohľady* LI, 10, 1935); *id.*, *Funkcie kroja na
moravskom Slovensku* (*Spisy národopisného odboru Matice slovenskej* I, Matica
Slovenská, 1937) (French résumé, pp. 68 ff.). Jan Mukařovský, *Estetická funkce*,

96]     It is true, in Saussure's *Cours* this general discipline is
thought of as erected on an essentially sociological and
psychological basis. At the same time, Saussure sketches something that can only be understood as a science of pure form, a
conception of language as an abstract transformation structure,
which he elucidates from a consideration of analogous structures.
Thus he sees that an essential trait—perhaps every essential
trait—of the semiological structure is rediscovered in the structures called *games*, for example in chess, to which he devotes
great attention. It is these considerations that must be brought
to the fore if we attempt to erect linguistics in the broader sense,
"semiology," on an *immanent* basis. And it is through these
considerations that both the possibility and the necessity will
arise of an intimate collaboration between linguistics and
logistics. It is precisely sign systems and game systems that
modern logicians have taken as their central subject, viewing
them as abstract transformation systems, and they have thereby
been led from their side to desire a study of language as well from
these points of view.[34]

In a new sense, then, it seems fruitful and necessary to establish a common point of view for a large number of disciplines,
from the study of literature, art, and music, and general history,
all the way to logistics and mathematics, so that from this common point of view these sciences are concentrated around a linguistically defined setting of problems. Each will be able to contribute in its own way to the general science of semiotics by
investigating to what extent and in what manner its objects may
be submitted to an analysis that is in agreement with the require-

*norma a hodnota jako sociální fakty* (*Fonction, norme et valeur esthétiques comme
faits sociaux*), Praha, 1936); *id.*, *L'art comme fait sémiologique* (*Actes du huitième
Congrès international de philosophie à Prague 2–7 septembre 1934*, Prague, 1936,
pp. 1065–1072). —A comprehensive attempt at a general semiology has been
made by E. Buyssens, *Les langages et le discours* (*Collection Lebègue*), Bruxelles,
1943.
[34] The principal work is Rudolf Carnap's *Logische Syntax der Sprache*, Wien,
1934; enlarged edition, *The Logical Syntax of Language*, 1937.

ments of linguistic theory. Thus new light might perhaps be cast on these disciplines, and they might be led to a critical self-examination. In this way, through a mutually fructifying collaboration, it should be possible to produce a general encyclopædia of sign structures.

Within this extraordinarily comprehensive sphere of problems, two particular questions are of special interest to us at the moment. First: What place within the totality of these semiotic structures can be thought of as assigned to language? Second: Where do the boundaries lie between semiotic and non-semiotic?

97]     A *language* may be defined as a paradigmatic whose paradigms are manifested by all purports, and a *text*, correspondingly, as a syntagmatic whose chains, if expanded indefinitely, are manifested by all purports. By a *purport* we understand a class of variables which manifest more than one chain under more than one syntagmatic, and/or more than one paradigm under more than one paradigmatic. In practice, a language is a semiotic into which all other semiotics may be translated—both all other languages, and all other conceivable semiotic structures. This translatability rests on the fact that languages, and they alone, are in a position to form any purport whatsoever;[35] in a language, and only in a language, we can "work over the inexpressible until it is expressed."[36] It is this quality that makes a language usable as a language, capable of giving satisfaction in any situation. There is no doubt that it rests on a structural peculiarity, on which we might be able to cast better light if we knew more about the specific structure of non-linguistic semiotics. It is an all but obvious conclusion that the basis lies in the unlimited possibility of forming signs and the

[35] We have made this observation independently of the Polish logician Alfred Tarski (*Studia philosophica* I, Lwów, 1935); see J. Jørgensen, *Træk af deduktionsteoriens udvikling i den nyere tid* (*Festskrift udg. af Københavns Universitet* nov. 1937), p. 15.

[36] Kierkegaard.

very free rules for forming units of great extension (sentences and the like) which are true of any language and which, on the other hand, make it possible for a language to allow false, inconsistent, imprecise, ugly, and unethical formulations as well as true, consistent, precise, beautiful, and ethical formulations. The grammatical rules of a language are independent of any scale of values, logical, æsthetic, or ethical; and, in general, a language is independent of any specific purpose.

If we wish to investigate the boundary between semiotic and non-semiotic, it is *a priori* an all but obvious conclusion that games lie close to that boundary, or perhaps on the boundary itself. In judging the structure of games, in comparison with semiotic structures that are not games, it is not uninteresting to compare the way in which game-structures have been considered up to now from the linguistic and from the logical side, independently of each other. From the logical side, importance has been attached to the fact that a game, chess for example, is a transformation system of essentially the same structure as a semiotic (*e.g.*, a mathematical semiotic), and the tendency 98] has been to consider the game as the simple model case, as normative for the concept of a semiotic. From the linguistic side, the analogy has been seen in the fact that a game is a system of values, analogous to economic values; and language and other value systems have been considered as normative for the concept of a game. The two ways of thinking have historical bases. The logistic theory of signs finds its starting-point in the metamathematics of Hilbert, whose idea was to consider the system of mathematical symbols as a system of expression-figuræ with complete disregard of their content, and to describe its transformation rules in the same way as one can describe the rules of a game, without considering possible interpretations. This method is carried over by the Polish logicians into their "metalogic" and is brought to its conclusion by Carnap in a sign-theory where, in principle, any semiotic is considered as a mere expression system without regard for the content. From this point of view it should be possible, in any meta-semiotic, *i.e.*, in any description of a semiotic, for an *inhaltliche Redeweise* to be replaced by a *formale Redeweise*.[37] The sign-theory of linguistics, on the other hand, has deep roots in the tradition according to which a sign is defined by its meaning. It is within this tradition that Saussure struggles with the problem. He makes it precise and justifies it by introducing the concept of value, a consequence of which is the recognition of the content-form and of the bilateral nature of the sign, leading to a theory of the sign that builds on the interplay between expression-form and content-form in the principle of commutation.

From the logical side, where the debate about the nature of the sign continues, the problem seems to be thought of as essentially a question of nominalism or realism.[38] For the linguistic theory of language, to which the present essay has made an introduction, this is not the question; it is rather a question of whether or not the *content-purport* need be involved in the sign-theory itself. Since the content-purport proves to be dispensable in the definition and description of a semiotic schema, a formal formulation and a nominalistic attitude are necessary and sufficient; on the other hand, the formal and nominalistic description in linguistic theory is not limited to the expression-form, but sees its object in the interplay between the expression-form and a *content-form*. Saussure's distinction between form and substance appears to be extraordinarily relevant for the present posing of the problem in logistics.

99]

On this basis logistics also may be led to see both differences and similarities between games and semiotics that are not games. The decisive point for the question of whether or not a sign is present is not whether it is interpreted, *i.e.*, whether a content-

---

[37] Introductory surveys of the development are given by J. Jørgensen, *op. cit.*; by L. Bloomfield, "Language or ideas?" (*Language* XII, 1936, pp. 89 ff.); and by Otto Neurath and Eino Kaila in the journal *Theoria* II, 1936, pp. 72 ff., 83 ff. See also G. H. von Wright, *Den logiska empirismen*, Stockholm, 1943.

[38] So U. Saarnio in the work cited on p. 61, note 13.

purport is ordered to it. In view of the selection between semiotic schema and semiotic usage there exist for the calculus of linguistic theory, not interpreted, but only interpretable, systems. In this respect, then, there is no difference between, *e.g.*, chess and pure algebra on the one hand and, *e.g.*, a language on the other. But when we wish to decide to what extent a game or other quasi-sign-systems, like pure algebra, are or are not semiotics, we must find out whether an exhaustive description of them necessitates operating with two planes, or whether the simplicity principle can be applied so far that operation with one plane is sufficient.

The prerequisite for the necessity of operating with two planes must be that the two planes, when they are tentatively set up, cannot be shown to have the same structure throughout, with a one-to-one relation between the functives of the one plane and the functives of the other. We shall express this by saying that the two planes must not be *conformal*. Two functives are said to be conformal if any particular derivate of the one functive without exception enters the same functions as a particular derivate of the other functive, and *vice versa*. We can accordingly set up the rule that two tentatively recognized components of one and the same class shall be reduced to one component if they are conformal and not commutable. The test which this rule institutes, and which we call the *derivate test*, is prescribed in linguistic theory for each individual stage of the textual analysis, coordinately with the commutation test; the two tests in conjunction are necessary to deduce whether or not a given object is a semiotic. We shall not enter here into the application of this derivate test to the higher-degree derivates of the semiotic (process), but shall consider only the first-degree derivates, the planes of the semiotic. These are not commutable, and the decisive factor as to whether they shall be treated as distinct or be identified with each other (in which latter case the applicability of linguistic theory to the given object ceases) is therefore solely whether they are conformal or not. Inductive experience shows

that for all hitherto observed languages the derivate test
100]    has negative result, and it will doubtless have negative
result for several other structures which till now have
been considered semiotics or which show by the derivate test
that they must be considered semiotics. But it seems just as
clear that the derivate test has positive result for many of the
structures which modern theory has favored calling semiotics.
This is easy to see in the case of pure games, in the interpretation
of which there is an entity of content corresponding to each
entity of expression (chess-piece or the like), so that if two planes
are tentatively posited the functional net will be entirely the
same in both. Such a structure, then, is not a semiotic, in the
sense given to the term by linguistic theory. We must leave it to
the specialists in the various fields to decide whether or not, for
example, the so-called symbolic systems of mathematics and
logic, or certain kinds of art, like music, are to be defined as
semiotics from this point of view. The possibility seems not to
be excluded that the logistic conception of a semiotic as mono-
planar is the result of having taken as point of departure (and
subsequently seeking a premature generalization therefrom)
structures which, according to our definition, are not semiotics
and which therefore diverge fundamentally from true semiotic
structures. It is proposed to use the name *symbolic systems* for
such structures as are interpretable (*i.e.*, to which a content-purport may be ordered) but not biplanar (*i.e.*, into which the simplicity principle does not permit us to encatalyze a content-
form). From the linguistic side there have been some misgivings
about applying the term *symbol* to entities that stand in a purely
arbitrary relation to their interpretation.[39] From this point of
view, *symbol* should be used only of entities that are isomorphic
with their interpretation, entities that are depictions or emblems,
like Thorvaldsen's Christ as a symbol for compassion, the ham-
mer and sickle as a symbol for Communism, scales as a symbol

[39] Thus Saussure, *Cours*, 2nd ed., p. 101, defines the symbol as non-arbitrary.

for justice, or the onomatopoetica in the sphere of language. But in logistics it is customary to use the word *symbol* in a far broader application, and it seems advantageous to be able to apply the word precisely to interpretable non-semiotic entities. There seems to be an essential affinity between the interpretable pieces of a game and isomorphic symbols, in that neither permits the further analysis into figuræ that is characteristic of signs. In the discussion that has taken place among linguists in recent years concerning the nature of the sign, attention has rightly been drawn to the agrammatical character of isomorphic symbols;[40] this is the same thought in a traditional formulation.

101]

### 22. *Connotative semiotics and metasemiotics*

In the preceding paragraphs, by a deliberate simplification, we have treated the "natural" language as the unique object of linguistic theory. In the last section, despite a considerable broadening of the perspective, we have still acted as if the unique object of linguistic theory were the *denotative semiotic*, by which we mean a semiotic none of whose planes is a semiotic. It still remains, through a final broadening of our horizon, to indicate that there are also semiotics whose expression plane is a semiotic and semiotics whose content plane is a semiotic. The former we shall call *connotative semiotics*, the latter *metasemiotics*. Since expression plane and content plane are defined only in opposition and in relation to each other, it follows that the definitions we have given here of connotative semiotics and metasemiotics are only provisional "real" definitions, to which we cannot ascribe even operative value.

When, in section 21, we defined *semiotic*, that definition did not concern the individual semiotic in contrast to other semiotics, but semiotics in contrast to non-semiotics, *i.e.*, *semiotic* as a higher hierarchial type, *la langue* as a concept or as a *class as one*. Of the individual semiotic in contrast to others, we know

[40] E. Buyssens, *Acta linguistica* II, 1940–41, p. 85.

that the linguistic theoretician foresees it in his calculus as a possible type of structure. On the other hand, we have not yet considered how the linguistic theoretician manages to recognize and identify the individual semiotic as such in his textual analysis. In preparing the analysis we have proceeded on the tacit assumption that the datum is a text composed in one definite semiotic, not in a mixture of two or more semiotics.

In other words, in order to establish a simple model situation we have worked with the premiss that the given text displays structural homogeneity, that we are justified in encatalyzing one and only one semiotic system to the text. This premiss, however, does not hold good in practice. On the contrary, any text 102] that is not of so small extension that it fails to yield a sufficient basis for deducing a system generalizable to other texts usually contains derivates that rest on different systems. Various parts, or parts of parts, of a text can be composed

1. in different *stylistic forms* (characterized by various restrictions: verse, prose, various blends of the two);
2. in different *styles* (creative style and the purely imitative, so-called normal, style; the creative and at the same time imitative style that is called archaizing);
3. in different *value-styles* (higher value-style and the lower, so-called vulgar, value-style; here also a neutral value-style that is considered neither as higher nor as lower);
4. in different *media* (speech, writing, gesture, flag code, *etc.*);
5. in different *tones* (angry, joyful, *etc.*);
6. in different *idioms*, under which must be distinguished
   a. different *vernaculars* (the common language of a community, jargons of various cliques or professions),
   b. different *national languages*,
   c. different *regional languages* (standard language, local dialect, *etc.*),
   d. different *physiognomies* (as concerns the expression, different "voices" or "organs").

Stylistic form, style, value-style, medium, tone, vernacular, national language, regional language, and physiognomy are solidary categories, so that any functive of denotative language must be defined in respect of them all at the same time. By combination of a member of one category with a member of another category arise hybrids, which often have, or can easily be provided with, special designations: belletristic style—a creative style that is a higher value-style;[41] slang—a creative style that is both a higher and a lower value-style; jargon and code—creative styles that are neither higher nor lower value-styles; colloquial language—a normal style that is neither a higher nor a lower value-style; lecture style—a higher value-style that is 103] speech and common language; pulpit style—a higher value-style that is speech and jargon; chancery style—a higher value-style that is an archaizing style, writing, and jargon; *etc.*

The purpose of these enumerations is not to exhaust, let alone formally define, these phenomena, but only to demonstrate their existence and variety.

The individual members of each of these classes and the units resulting from their combination we shall call *connotators*. Some of these connotators may be solidary with certain systems of semiotic schemata, others with certain systems of semiotic usage, and others with both. This is impossible to know *a priori*, since the situation changes. To name only possibilities that may appear extreme, it is impossible to know beforehand whether a physiognomy (one person's utterances as opposed to another's) represents only a specific usage and not also a specific schema (differing perhaps only slightly from another, but still differing),

---

[41] A *jargon* in the more general sense can be characterized as a neutral value-style with specific signs (usually: sign-expressions), a *code* as a neutral value-style with specific expression-manifestations. Using the designation *genre-style* of an idiom that is solidary with certain literary genres (typical examples are certain Ancient Greek dialects), we can characterize a *terminology* as being both a jargon and a genre-style, and a *scientific semiotic* (insofar as it is not a system of symbols, in our sense) as being both a code and a genre-style.

or whether a national language represents a specific linguistic schema or, in comparison with another national language, only represents a specific linguistic usage while the schemata of the two national languages are identical.

To ensure a self-consistent and exhaustive description, linguistic theory must therefore prescribe such a procedure for textual analysis as will enable us to keep these cases apart. Strangely enough, in previous linguistics attention has been paid to this requirement only to a very slight degree. The explanation is partly to be sought in the fact that transcendent points of view have been assumed. For example, it has been thought possible to establish from a vague sociological starting-point the (in all reasonable probability false) postulate that the existence of a social norm implies that a national language is also uniform and specific in its internal structure and that, on the other hand, a linguistic physiognomy *qua* physiognomy is a *quantité négligeable* and can be taken indiscriminately without further ado as representative of a national language. Only the London school has been consciously cautious on this point: Daniel Jones' definition of the phoneme expressly refers to "the pronunciation of one individual speaking in a definite style."[42]

104]     Given unrestrictedness (productivity) of the text, there will always be "translatability," which here means expression-substitution, between two signs each belonging to a sign-class of its own, this sign-class in its turn being solidary with its respective connotator. This criterion is especially obvious and easily applicable to the signs of great extension which textual analysis encounters in its earliest operations: any textual derivate (*e.g.*, chapter) can be translated from one stylistic form, style, value-style, medium, tone, vernacular, national or regional language, physiognomy to another. As we have seen, this translatability is not always reciprocal if any other semiotic is concerned than a language, but if a language is included, a uni-

---

[42] See p. 64, note 17, and also, in particular, D. Jones, *Travaux du Cercle linguistique de Prague* IV, 1931, p. 74.

lateral translatability is always possible. In the textual analysis, consequently, *connotators* will appear as parts that enter into functives in such a way that the functives have mutual substitution when these parts are deducted; and under certain conditions connotators are found in all the functives of a given degree. But this is still insufficient to define a connotator. We call an entity that has the given property an *indicator*, and we must distinguish between two kinds of indicators: *signals* (see p. 72) and *connotators*. The difference between them from an operative point of view is that a signal may always be referred unambiguously to one definite plane of the semiotic, while this is never so of a connotator. A *connotator*, then, is an indicator which is found, under certain conditions, in both planes of the semiotic.

In the textual analysis the connotators must be disengaged from the deduction. In this way those signs which are different only by being solidary each with its own connotator appear as varieties. These varieties, in contrast to ordinary variants (p. 81), are particular and must be handled differently in the further analysis. In this way we protect ourselves against mixing together different semiotic schemata (and usages); if there should later prove to be identity, this will easily appear from a mapping.

But it is clear that the connotators themselves also provide an object whose treatment belongs to semiotics. Their treatment does not fall to the discipline that analyzes denotative semiotics; the only task of that discipline is to sort out the connotators and keep them collected for later treatment. This treatment belongs to a special discipline which determines the study of denotative semiotics.

Now it seems obvious that the solidarity which exists 105] between certain sign classes and certain connotators is a *sign function*, since the sign classes are *expression* for the connotators as *content*. Thus it is the semiotic schema(ta) and usage(s) which we designate as the Danish language that are *expression for* the connotator "Danish." Likewise it is the semiotic schema(ta) and usage(s) which we designate as the linguistic physiognomy N. N. that are *expression for* the real physiognomy N.N. (that person), and correspondingly in all other cases. Not for nothing does the national language stand as "symbol" for the nation, the local dialect as "symbol" for the region, *etc.*

Thus it seems appropriate to view the connotators as content for which the denotative semiotics are expression, and to designate this content and this expression as a *semiotic*, namely a *connotative semiotic*. In other words, after the analysis of the denotative semiotic is completed, the connotative semiotic must be subjected to an analysis according to just the same procedure. Here again it will be necessary to distinguish between a semiotic schema and a usage. The connotators will have to be analyzed on the basis of their mutual functions, not on the basis of the content-purport that is or can be ordered to them. Thus the study of the schema of a connotative semiotic does not treat the actual notions of social or sacral character that common usage attaches to concepts like national language, local dialect, jargon, stylistic form, *etc.* But to this study of the schema of a connotative semiotic it will be necessary to order a study of its usage, quite as for a denotative semiotic.

Thus a connotative semiotic is a semiotic that is not a language, and one whose expression plane is provided by the content plane and expression plane of a denotative semiotic. Thus it is a semiotic one plane of which (namely the expression plane) is a semiotic.

What may be particularly surprising here is that we have discovered a semiotic whose *expression plane* is a semiotic. For, after the development taken by logistics in the work of the Polish logicians, one is prepared for the existence of a semiotic whose *content plane* is a semiotic. This is the so-called metalanguage[43] (or, we should say, *metasemiotic*), by which is meant a semiotic

---

[43] See J. Jørgensen's presentation (referred to on page 109, note 35), pp. 9 ff.

that treats of a semiotic; in our terminology this must mean a semiotic whose content is a semiotic. Such a metasemiotic linguistics itself must be.

106]     Now, as already remarked, the concepts of expression and content are not well suited to be the basis of formal definitions because expression and content are arbitrarily assigned designations for elements that are defined only oppositively and negatively. We shall therefore define on another basis, and first articulate the class of semiotics into a class of scientific semiotics and a class of non-scientific semiotics. For this we need the concept of *operation*, which we have defined earlier. By a *scientific semiotic*[44] we mean a semiotic that is an operation; by a *non-scientific semiotic* we understand a semiotic that is not an operation. We accordingly define a *connotative semiotic* as a non-scientific semiotic one or more of whose planes is (are) (a) semiotic(s), and a *metasemiotic* as a scientific semiotic one or more of whose planes is (are) (a) semiotic(s). The case that usually occurs in practice is, as we have seen, that *one* of the planes is a semiotic.

Since, now, as the logicians have pointed out, we can further imagine a scientific semiotic that treats of a metasemiotic, we can, in conformity with their terminology, define a *meta-(scientific semiotic)* as a metasemiotic with a scientific semiotic as an object semiotic (a semiotic that enters as a plane into a semiotic is said to be an *object semiotic* of that semiotic). In conformity with Saussure's terminology we can define a *semiology* as a metasemiotic with a non-scientific semiotic as an object semiotic. And finally, we can use the designation *metasemiology* of a meta-(scientific semiotic) whose object semiotics are semiologies.

In order to clarify not only the basis of linguistics but also its remotest consequences linguistic theory is obliged to add to the

---

[44] The reason for our not simply saying *science* lies in the fact that we must reckon with the possibility of certain sciences' not being semiotics in our sense but symbolic systems.

study of denotative semiotics a study of connotative semiotics and of metasemiologies. This obligation rests with our special science because it can be resolved satisfactorily only from premisses peculiar to the science.

Our last task must then consist in considering how *metasemiology* is appropriately organized from the linguistic point of view.

Usually a metasemiotic will be (or can be) wholly or partly identical with its object semiotic. Thus the linguist who describes a language will himself be able to use that language in the description; likewise, the semiologist who describes semiotics that are not languages will be able to make that description in a language; should this not be the case, the semiotic that is used will in any event always be translatable into a language (*cf.* the definition of a language). From this it follows that 107] metasemiology, if it is to yield a complete description of the semiotic of semiology, must in very great part repeat the proper results of semiology. The simplicity principle, however, enjoins us to follow a method of procedure that will enable us to avoid this; from considerations of appropriateness we must so organize metasemiology that in practice its object is distinct from that of semiology; and we must behave correspondingly in the face of eventual metasemiologies of higher order, and not add further metasemiologies of still higher order whose objects would be no different from those already treated.

Metasemiology must therefore direct its interest, not toward the language, already described by semiology, which semiology uses, but toward the eventual modifications of it or additions to it which semiology has introduced to produce its special jargon. And it is likewise clear that metasemiology must not yield a description of the propositions that enter into the theory of semiology, if it can prove that these propositions are possible units that could already be foreseen from the system of the language. Its sphere is, on the contrary, the special *terminology* of semiology, and here it will find that three different kinds of terms are used:

1. Terms that enter as definienda in the definition system of semiology, and whose content is therefore already defined, *i.e.*, analyzed (*cf*. p. 72), by semiology itself. These terms do not fall in the special sphere of metasemiology.

2. Terms that are taken over from a language and enter as indefinables into the definition system of semiology. Such indefinables occupy, in contrast to the situation in other sciences, a peculiar place in semiology: since these indefinables are drawn from the object language of semiology, semiology in its analysis of the content plane will have produced a definition of them. Neither do these terms fall in the special sphere of metasemiology.

3. Terms that are not taken over from a language (but which still must be required to have an expression-structure agreeing with the system of the language) and which enter as indefinables into the propositions of semiology. Under this heading we must distinguish between two kinds of terms:

108]    a. Terms for highest-degree variations of highest-degree invariants, *i.e.*, highest-degree glosseme-variations (and signal-variations), the ultimate and "smallest" variations (individuals and/or localized variations), which semiology has come to treat in the course of its analysis. These variations necessarily remain as indefinables for semiology, since definition means analysis and analysis within semiology is impossible at precisely this spot. On the other hand, an analysis of these variations is possible within metasemiology, since there they must be described as the minimal signs that enter into semiology, and be analyzed in the same way as semiology analyzes the minimal signs of a language, *i.e.*, through a resolution into figuræ on the basis of a commutation test set up for the semiotic of semiology, and through an articulation into variants. It will be seen that the entities that enter as variants into the content plane and expression plane in a language (or, in general, into the 1st-order object semiotic) will be invariants in the content plane in semiology.

b. Terms for categories of variants and of invariants. Their contents, viewed as *class as one*, will be syncretisms of the entities discussed under (a) or of syncretisms of them.

The task of metasemiology is consequently to subject the minimal signs of semiology, whose content is identical with the ultimate content- and expression-variants of the object semiotic (language), to a relational analysis according to the same procedure as is generally prescribed for the textual analysis. As in ordinary textual analysis, so here there shall be an attempt to register to the widest possible extent the realized entities, *i.e.*, the entities accessible to *particular* division.

To understand what may here take place, one must remember that we have not been able to maintain unmodified Saussure's distinction between form and substance but that this difference has proved to be in reality a difference between two forms within different hierarchies. A functive, *e.g.*, in a language, can be viewed as a linguistic form or as a purport-form; from these two different ways of viewing things there arise two different objects, which yet may also be said in a certain sense to be identical since only the point of view from which they are seen is different. Saussure's distinction, and the formulation he has given to it, must therefore not deceive us into believing that the functives which we discover through an analysis of a linguistic 109] schema cannot with some right be said to be of a physical nature. They may very well be said to be physical entities (or syncretisms thereof) which are defined by mutual function. Therefore with the same right the metasemiological analysis of the content of the minimal signs of semiology may be said to be an analysis of physical entities that are defined by mutual function. To what extent it is possible to consider ultimately all entities in any semiotic whatsoever, in its content and expression, as physical or reducible to the physical is a purely epistemological question of physicalism *contra* phenomenalism.

This question has been the object of a debate[45] on which we shall not here take a position and on which the theory of the linguistic schema need not take a stand. In the present linguistic debate, on the other hand, it has often been possible to detect a certain inclination, among both the adherents and the opponents of the glossematic point of view, to misunderstand the question, as if the object which the linguist analyzes by encatalysis of a linguistic form could not be of a physical nature just as well as the object which the "investigator of the substance" must analyze by encatalysis of one or another "non-linguistic" purport-form. But it is necessary to overcome this misunderstanding if one is to understand the task of metasemiology. Metasemiology, by the displacement in point of view which the transition from an object semiotic to its metasemiotic involves, puts new means in hand for taking up again, with the help of the usual semiological methods, and for carrying further the analysis which from the point of view of semiology was exhausted. This can only mean that the ultimate variants of a language are subjected to a further, particular analysis on a completely physical basis. *In other words, metasemiology is in practice identical with the so-called description of substance.* The task of metasemiology is to undertake a self-consistent, exhaustive, and simplest possible analysis of the *things* which appeared for semiology as irreducible individuals (or localized entities) of content and of the *sounds* (or written marks, *etc.*) which appeared for semiology as irreducible individuals (or localized entities) of expression. Metasemiological analysis will have to be carried out on the basis of the functions and according to the already indicated procedure, until the analysis is exhausted and
110]    until we have reached, here also, the ultimate variants in the face of which the point of view of cohesion is no longer fruitful, and where the sought-for clarification by reasons

---

[45] On this point see, in addition to the works of Bloomfield and Neurath (p. 111, note 37), Alf Ross, "On the Illusion of Consciousness" (*Theoria* VII, 1941, pp. 171 ff.).

and causes must give way to a purely statistical description as the only possible one (*cf.* p. 84): the final situation of physics and deductive phonetics.

It is immediately obvious that there can and must also be added to the connotative semiotic a metasemiotic, which further analyzes the final objects of the connotative semiotic. Just as the metasemiology of denotative semiotics will in practice treat the objects of phonetics and semantics in a reinterpreted form, so in the metasemiotic of connotative semiotics the largest parts of specifically sociological linguistics and Saussurean external linguistics will find their place in reinterpreted form. To this metasemiotic belongs the task of analyzing various—geographical and historical, political and social, sacral, psychological—content-purports that are attached to nation (as content for national language), region (as content for regional language), the value-forms of styles, personality (as content for physiognomy; essentially a task for individual psychology), mood, *etc.* Many special sciences, in the first place, presumably, sociology, ethnology and psychology, must be thought of as making their contribution here.

In deference to the simplicity principle, metasemiologies of higher orders, on the other hand, must not be set up, since, if they are tentatively carried out, they will not bring any other results than those already achieved in the metasemiology of the first order or before.

## 23. *Final perspective*

The restricted practical and technical attitude which is often natural for the specialist at work and which in the domain of linguistics leads to formulating the demand for linguistic theory simply as a demand for a sure method of describing a given limited text composed in a previously defined "natural" language, has, in the course of our presentation, with logical necessity, had to make way step by step for an ever broader scientific and ever broader humanistic attitude, until the idea finally comes to rest in a totality-concept that can scarcely be imagined more absolute.

The individual act of speech obliges the investigator 111]    to encatalyze a system cohesive with it, the individual physiognomy is a totality which it is incumbent on the linguist to know through analysis and synthesis—but not a closed totality. It is a totality with outward cohesions which oblige us to encatalyze other linguistic schemata and usages, from which alone it is possible to throw light on the individual peculiarity of the physiognomy; and it is a totality with inward cohesions with a connotative purport that explains the totality in its unity and in its variety. For local dialect and style, speech and writing, languages and other semiotics, this procedure is repeated in ever larger circles. The smallest system is a self-sufficient totality, but no totality is isolated. Catalysis on catalysis oblige us to extend the field of vision until all cohesions are exhaustively accounted for. It is not the individual language alone that is the object of the linguist, but the whole class of languages, the members of which are connected with each other and explain and cast light on each other. It is impossible to draw a boundary between the study of the individual linguistic type and the general typology of languages; the individual linguistic type is a special case within that typology and, like all functives, has its existence only by virtue of the function that connects it with others. In the calculative typology of linguistic theory all linguistic schemata are foreseen; they constitute a system with correlations between the individual members. Relations, also, may be observed; they are the contacts between languages that are manifested partly as loan-contacts, partly as genetic linguistic relationships, and which independently of the linguistic types produce linguistic families; these relations, too, like all others, depend on a pure presupposition, which—quite like the relation between the parts of the textual process—is manifested in time but is not itself defined by time.

Through further catalysis connotative semiotic, metasemiotic, and metasemiology are necessarily drawn into the picture. Thus all those entities which in the first instance, with the pure consideration of the schema of the object semiotic, had to be provisionally eliminated as non-semiotic elements, are reintroduced as necessary components into semiotic structures of a higher order. Accordingly, we find no non-semiotics that are not components of semiotics, and, in the final instance, no object that is not illuminated from the key position of linguistic theory. Semiotic structure is revealed as a stand from which all scientific objects may be viewed.

Linguistic theory here takes up in an undreamed-of way and in undreamed-of measure the duties that it imposed on itself (pp. 8, 19–20). In its point of departure linguistic theory was established as immanent, with constancy, system, and internal

112] function as its sole aims, to the apparent cost of fluctuation and nuance, life and concrete physical and phenomenological reality. A temporary restriction of the field of vision was the price that had to be paid to elicit from language itself its secret. But precisely through that immanent point of view and by virtue of it, language itself returns the price that it demanded. In a higher sense than in linguistics till now, language has again become a key-position in knowledge. Instead of hindering transcendence, immanence has given it a new and better basis; immanence and transcendence are joined in a higher unity on the basis of immanence. Linguistic theory is led by an inner necessity to recognize not merely the linguistic system, in its schema and in its usage, in its totality and in its individuality, but also man and human society behind language, and all man's sphere of knowledge through language. At that point linguistic theory has reached its prescribed goal:

*humanitas et universitas*

# ALPHABETIC REGISTER
# OF DEFINED TERMS

# DEFINITIONS

Terms are given in both English and Danish. Numerals in parentheses following the definitions refer to other, explicitly premised definitions.

1. Analysis—*Analyse:* description of an object by the uniform dependences of other objects on it and on each other.
2. Class—*Klasse:* object that is subjected to analysis. (1)
3. Components—*Afsnit:* objects that are registered by a single analysis as uniformly dependent on the class and on each other. (1, 2)
4. Hierarchy—*Hierarki:* class of classes. (2)
5. Analysis complex—*Inddelingskompleks:* class of analyses of one and the same class. (1, 2)
6. Operation—*Operation:* description that is in agreement with the empirical principle.
7. Synthesis—*Syntese:* description of an object as a component of a class. (2, 3)
8. Function—*Funktion:* dependence that fulfils the conditions for an analysis. (1)
9. Functive—*Funktiv:* object that has function to other objects. (8)
10. Contract—*Indgaa:* A functive is said to *contract* its function. (8, 9)
11. Entity—*Størrelse:* functive that is not a function. (8, 9)
12. Constant—*Konstant:* functive whose presence is a necessary condition for the presence of the functive to which it has function. (8, 9)
13. Variable—*Variabel:* functive whose presence is not a necessary condition for the presence of the functive to which it has function. (8, 9)

14. Interdependence—*Interdependens:* function between two constants. (8, 12)

15. Determination—*Determination:* function between a constant and a variable. (8, 12, 13)

16. Constellation—*Konstellation:* function between two variables. (8, 13)

17. Cohesion—*Kohæsion:* function among whose functives appear one or more constants. (8, 9, 12)

18. Reciprocity—*Reciprocitet:* function containing either only constants or only variables. (8, 12, 13)

19. Deduction—*Deduktion:* continued analysis or analysis complex with determination between the analyses that enter therein. (1, 5, 15)

20. Procedure—*Procedure:* class of operations with mutual determination. (2, 6, 15)

21. Derivates—*Derivater:* components and components-of-components of a class within one and the same deduction (2, 3, 19)

22. Include—*Indbefatte:* A class is said to *include* its derivates. (2, 21)

23. Enter into—*Indgaa i:* Derivates are said to *enter into* their class. (2, 21)

24. Degree—*Grad:* reference to the number of the classes through which derivates are dependent on their lowest common class. (If this number is 0, the derivates are said to be of the 1st degree; if the number is 1, the derivates are said to be of the 2nd degree; and so forth.) (2, 21)

25. Induction—*Induktion:* continued synthesis with determination between the syntheses that enter therein. (7, 15, 23)

26. Correlation—*Korrelation:* either-or function. (8)

27. Relation—*Relation:* both-and function. (8)

28. System—*System:* correlational hierarchy. (4, 26)

29. Process—*Forløb:* relational hierarchy. (4, 27)

30. Articulation—*Leddeling:* analysis of a system. (1, 28)

31. Partition—*Deling:* analysis of a process. (1, 29)

32. Universality—*Universalitet:* An operation with a given result is called *universal,* and its resultants *universals,* if it is asserted that the operation can be performed on any object whatsoever. (6)

33. Particularity—*Partikularitet:* An operation with a given result is called *particular,* and its resultants *particulars,* if it is asserted that the operation can be performed on a certain object but not on any other object. (6)

34. Realization—*Realisation:* A class is said to be *realized* if it can be taken as the object of a particular analysis. (1, 2, 33)

35. Virtuality—*Virtualitet:* A class is said to be *virtual* if it cannot be taken as the object of a particular analysis. (1, 2, 33)

36. Complementarity—*Komplementaritet:* interdependence between terms in a system. (14, 28)

37. Solidarity—*Solidaritet:* interdependence between terms in a process. (14, 29)

38. Specification—*Specifikation:* determination between terms in a system. (15, 28)

39. Selection—*Selektion:* determination between terms in a process. (15, 29)

40. Autonomy—*Autonomi:* constellation within a system. (16, 28)

41. Combination—*Kombination:* constellation within a process. (16, 29)

42. Definition—*Definition:* partition of a sign-content or of a sign-expression. (31)

43. Rank—*Række:* Derivates of the same degree belonging to one and the same process or to one and the same system are said to constitute a *rank.* (21, 24, 28, 29)

44. Mutation—*Mutation:* function existing between first-degree derivates of one and the same class; a function that

has relation to a function between other first-degree derivates of one and the same class and belonging to the same
rank. (2, 8, 21, 24, 27, 43)

45. Sum—*Sum:* class that has function to one or more other
classes within the same rank. (2, 8, 43)

46. Establishment—*Etablering:* relation that exists between a
sum and a function entering into it. The function is said
to *establish* the sum, and the sum to *be established by* the
function. (8, 23, 27, 45)

47. Application—*Ikrafttræden:* Given a functive that is present
under certain conditions and absent under certain other
conditions, then, under the conditions where the functive
is present, there is said to be *application* of the functive,
and under these conditions the functive is said to *apply.* (9)

48. Suspension—*Suspension:* Given a functive that is present
under certain conditions and absent under certain other
conditions, then, under the conditions where the functive
is absent, there is said to be *suspension* of the functive, and
under these conditions the functive is said to *be suspended.*
(9)

49. Overlapping—*Overlapping:* suspended mutation between
two functives. (9, 44, 48)

50. Manifestation—*Manifestation:* selection between hierarchies and between derivates of different hierarchies.
(4, 21, 39)

51. Form—*Form:* the constant in a manifestation. (12, 50)

52. Substance—*Substans:* the variable in a manifestation.
(13, 50)

53. Semiotic—*Semiotik:* hierarchy, any of whose components
admits of a further analysis into classes defined by mutual
relation, so that any of these classes admits of an analysis
into derivates defined by mutual mutation. (1, 2, 3, 4,
21, 27, 44)

54. Paradigm—*Paradigme:* class within a semiotic system. (2,
28, 53)

55. Chain—*Kæde:* class within a semiotic process. (2, 29, 53)

56. Member—*Led:* component of a paradigm. (3, 54)

57. Part—*Del:* component of a chain. (3, 55)

58. Semiotic schema—*Semiotisk sprogbygning:* form that is a semiotic. (51, 53)

59. Commutation—*Kommutation:* mutation between the members of a paradigm. (44, 54, 56)

60. Permutation—*Permutation:* mutation between the parts of a chain. (44, 55, 57)

61. Words—*Ord:* minimal permutable signs. (60)

62. Substitution—*Substitution:* absence of mutation between the members of a paradigm. (44, 54, 56)

63. Invariants—*Invarianter:* correlates with mutual commutation. (26, 59)

64. Variants—*Varianter:* correlates with mutual substitution. (26, 62)

65. Glossemes—*Glossemer:* minimal forms which the theory leads us to establish as bases of explanation, the irreducible invariants. (63)

66. Semiotic usage—*Usus:* substance that manifests a semiotic schema. (50, 52, 58)

67. Paradigmatic—*Paradigmatik:* semiotic system. (28, 53)

68. Syntagmatic—*Syntagmatik:* semiotic process. (29, 53)

69. Purport—*Mening:* class of variables which manifest more than one chain under more than one syntagmatic, and/or more than one paradigm under more than one paradigmatic. (2, 13, 50, 54, 55, 67, 68)

70. Variations—*Variationer:* combined variants. (41, 64)

71. Varieties—*Varieteter:* solidary variants. (37, 64)

72. Individual—*Individ:* variation that cannot be further articulated into variations. (30, 70)

73. Localized (variety)—*Lokaliseret:* variety that cannot be further articulated into varieties. (30, 71)

74. Unit—*Enhed:* syntagmatic sum. (45, 68)

75. Category—*Kategori:* paradigm that has correlation to one

or more other paradigms within the same rank. (26, 43, 54)

76. Functional category—*Funktionskategori:* category of the functives that are registered in a single analysis with a given function taken as the basis of analysis. (1, 8, 9, 75)

77. Functival category—*Funktivkategori:* category that is registered by articulation of a functional category according to functival possibilities. (9, 30, 75, 76)

78. Syncretism—*Synkretisme:* category that is established by an overlapping. (46, 49, 75)

79. Dominance—*Dominans:* solidarity between a variant on the one hand and an overlapping on the other hand. (37, 49, 64)

80. Obligatory (dominance)—*Obligatorisk:* dominance in which the dominant in respect of the syncretism is a variety. (71, 78, 79)

81. Optional (dominance)—*Valgfri:* dominance in which the dominant in respect of the syncretism is a variation. (70, 78, 79)

82. Facultativity—*Fakultativitet:* overlapping with zero in which the dominance is optional. (49, 79, 81)

83. Fusion—*Sammenfald:* manifestation of a syncretism which, from the point of view of the substance hierarchy, is identical with the manifestation of all or none of the functives that enter into the syncretism. (4, 9, 23, 50, 52, 78)

84. Implication—*Implikation:* manifestation of a syncretism which, from the point of view of the substance hierarchy, is identical with the manifestation of one or more of the functives that enter into the syncretism but not with all. (4, 9, 23, 50, 52, 78)

85. Resolution—*Opløsning:* To *resolve* a syncretism means to introduce the syncretism-variety which does not contract the overlapping that establishes the syncretism. (10, 46, 49, 71, 78)

86. Concept—*Begreb:* syncretism between things. (78)

87. Latency—*Latens:* overlapping with zero in which the dominance is obligatory. (49, 79, 80)

88. Catalysis—*Katalyse:* registration of cohesions through the replacement of one entity by another to which it has substitution. (11, 17, 62)

89. Language—*Sprog:* paradigmatic whose paradigms are manifested by all purports. (50, 54, 67, 69)

90. Text—*Text:* syntagmatic whose chains, if expanded indefinitely, are manifested by all purports. (50, 55, 68, 69)

91. Linguistic schema—*Sprogbygning:* form that is a language. (51, 89)

92. Linguistic usage—*Sprogbrug:* substance that manifests a linguistic schema. (50, 52, 91)

93. Element—*Element:* member of a functival category. (56, 77)

94. Taxeme—*Taxem:* virtual element yielded at the stage of analysis where selection is used for the last time as the basis of analysis. (1, 35, 39, 93)

95. Connective —*Konnektiv:* functive that under certain conditions is solidary with complex units of a certain degree. (9, 24, 37, 74)

96. Conformity—*Konformitet:* Two functives are said to be *conformal* if any particular derivate of the one functive without exception contracts the same functions as a particular derivate of the other functive, and *vice versa.* (8, 9, 10, 21, 33)

97. Symbolic systems—*Symbolsystemer:* structures to which a content-purport may be ordered but into which the simplicity principle does not permit us to encatalyze a content-form. (51, 69, 88)

98. Denotative semiotic—*Denotationssemiotik:* semiotic none of whose planes is a semiotic. (53)

99. Indicators—*Indikatorer:* parts that enter into functives in such a way that the functives have mutual substitution when these parts are deducted. (9, 23, 57, 62)

100. Signal—*Signal:* indicator that may always be referred unambiguously to one definite plane of the semiotic. (53, 99)

101. Connotator—*Konnotator:* indicator which is found, under

certain conditions, in both planes of the semiotic. (53, 99)

102. Scientific semiotic—*Videnskabssemiotik:* semiotic that is an operation. (6, 53)

103. Connotative semiotic—*Konnotationssemiotik:* non-scientific semiotic one or more of whose planes is (are) (a) semiotic(s). (53, 102)

104. Metasemiotic—*Metasemiotik:* scientific semiotic one or more of whose planes is (are) (a) semiotic(s). (53, 102)

105. Object semiotic—*Objektsemiotik:* semiotic that enters as a plane into a semiotic. (53)

106. Meta-(scientific semiotic)—*Metavidenskabssemiotik:* meta-semiotic with a scientific semiotic as an object semiotic. (102, 104, 105)

107. Semiology—*Semiologi:* metasemiotic with a non-scientific semiotic as an object semiotic. (102, 104, 105)

108. Metasemiology—*Metasemiologi:* meta-(scientific semiotic) whose object semiotics are semiologies. (105, 106, 107)

# INDEX

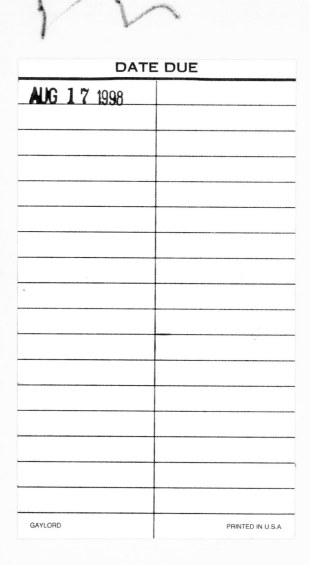

## DATE DUE

| AUG 17 1998 | |
|---|---|
| | |
| | |
| | |
| | |
| | |
| | |
| | |
| | |
| | |
| | |
| | |
| | |
| | |
| | |
| | |
| | |